In the Mill

By JOHN MASEFIELD

Author of "The Nine Days Wonder,"
"The Bird of Dawning," etc.

THIS chapter from the youth of England's Poet Laureate is an unusual and very pleasant bit of literary autobiography.

It was during his two years in a carpet mill (in Yonkers, New York) that the budding poet first entered into the realms of gold. Before that ships and farms had given him little time for reading or writing; now free evenings, Sundays and holidays were a boon. Here he discovered Keats and Shelley, and the Pre-Raphaelites; devoured Chaucer, Shakespeare, and Milton; and delved into much trash as well.

It is a nostalgic book, memories of a brief but very significant period. Masefield's fellow workers although friendly to him, had strange and hostile notions about the English, which leads to speculative comment. Sundays the young man liked to row across the Hudson and ramble over the Palisades, then a wilderness. His attempts at writing in both prose and verse began at this *time* and it finally came to him that *the place for* him was London even *if he starved* in a garret there. So he *signed for a* last voyage homewar*d, outward* bound also on a liter*ary career—* what results the world knows.

IN THE MILL

THE MACMILLAN COMPANY
NEW YORK · BOSTON · CHICAGO
DALLAS · ATLANTA · SAN FRANCISCO

MACMILLAN AND CO., LIMITED
LONDON · BOMBAY · CALCUTTA
MADRAS · MELBOURNE

**THE MACMILLAN COMPANY
OF CANADA, LIMITED**
TORONTO

JOHN MASEFIELD

◇◇◇◇◇◇◇◇◇◇◇◇◇◇◇◇◇◇◇◇◇◇◇◇◇◇◇◇◇◇◇◇◇◇◇◇◇◇◇

IN

THE

MILL

◇◇◇◇◇◇◇◇◇◇◇◇◇◇◇◇◇◇◇◇◇◇◇◇◇◇◇◇◇◇◇◇◇◇◇◇◇

New York

THE MACMILLAN COMPANY

1941

Copyright, 1941, by

JOHN MASEFIELD

First Printing

PRINTED IN THE UNITED STATES OF AMERICA
BY THE VAIL-BALLOU PRESS, INC., BINGHAMTON, N. Y.

To my old companions

ANTY
BILLY
DUNK
ED
EDDIE
JACOB
JIMMY
PAT
PERCE
SMIDDY
&
TOMMY

"Therefore . . . dwell as having refuges in yourselves, resorts in yourselves and not elsewhere. . . . Whoever shall dwell as having refuges in themselves . . . shall reach to the limit of darkness, whoever are desirous of learning."

GAUTAMA BUDDHA TO ĀNANDA

The Life of Buddha, by Edward J. Thomas
(Kegan Paul. 1931)

IN THE MILL

THOUGH I had not gone to bed till after midnight, I must have been called at five o'clock. Coming downstairs, I found my two fellow-workers waiting for me. One of these was Johnny, the other John-na.

Johnny was a short, stocky humorous fellow, who thought that the country was going through a crisis; John-na was a big Italian, something of an artist in his way, who, at one time, had been taught to sing. He was always singing to himself at his work in a little low voice from a great repertory of odds and ends of song. Usually, he was a merry man, easy to get along with; but the word went about, that one should be cautious with John-na, for he carried a knife in his boot and was very quick with it when vexed. They had a breakfast for me there, and chaffed me, as I ate, about the disasters to which I was going. When we parted, John-na gave me a packet of lunch to take with me, and Johnny gave me an envelope full of cigars. I liked both men, and was sorry to say good-bye to them. I was to see John-na several times after that, but I never saw Johnny again.

With my bag, I went out into the September dawn, and took the Elevated Railway to 155th Street, where I took train to Yonkers.

All this was more than forty-five years ago, when Upper New York was still uncleared and unbuilt. From 155th Street one passed into the woodland which was much as it had been when the Red Indians had it. Here and there in the woodland were pretty little hamlets; near the River there was modern industry; elsewhere the land seemed untamed, uncleared, untouched by man; the grey rock stood up among the sumachs and the maples; all was Nature's still, man had not fenced it into bits and called it his.

At Yonkers, then, one came downstairs from the Depot into the end of the Square, from which five or six main roads run. A friend was waiting for me there. I left my bag at the house where I was to stay (it was only one minute's walk from the Depot) and then crossed the Square with my friend to the Restaurant for a cup of coffee. The Restaurant was famous throughout Yonkers. It was always crowded. Even at that early hour, it was full of clients. The

waiters were all men of colour, about as dark as dark
honey.   They were excellent at their job, swift and
sure, like negro boxers, and at all times smiling and
ready for a joke.   They had a jargon of their own
with which they shouted orders to the kitchens.

"Draw One.   Draw Two.   Boil Three on One.
Boil six on three.   Two hams AND.   Draw One.
Smash four on two.   Ham-AND.   Three Bucks.
Ham AND.   LivrAND RARE.   Porter RARE.
Draw One.   Boil four on two.   HamAnd.   Bucks
and PASS de Maypole."

Draw One was Coffee.   Draw Two was tea.   The
coffee, as always in America, was very good indeed.
At the Cash-desk, the Proprietor leaned, always watch-
ful, always smiling.   He thoroughly enjoyed his work;
he had made the place from its beginnings and knew
every client; to each client, once in each week, he gave
a cigar.

But on this morning, I drank my coffee, and set out
with my friend on my first walk to the mills, rather
more than a mile away.   As we left the Restaurant, I
had my first view of the Hudson River, with the Palisades on the Jersey shore.   The beauty of the sight
took my breath away.

"What are those cliffs?"

"The Palisades.   They run for miles, both up and
down."

"Can I get a boat and go over to them?"

"Sure."

Soon after we had left the Square, we passed some
red brick buildings on the left-hand side of the road.
"Those are the Designing Rooms" my friend said, "and
Offices and general headquarters." A little further on,
we turned into a great road in which trolley tram-cars
were running; the road was crowded with people all
moving as we were moving, northwards. A lithe, active man joined us here, an old friend of my friend; we
went on together; sometimes as we went my companions hailed or were hailed. We crossed a little river,
the Nepperhan, and soon came upon the expanse of
the mills, in front and to the right of us. My friend
pointed to the right to stretches of red brick building.
"Those are all parts of it," he said. "They're mostly
Hungarians in these parts. All the early processes are
done here. You won't have anything to do with any
of these. Some of the Hungarians are a pretty tough
lot."

They had that name, throughout my stay, but I
never met any of them, and never entered any of the
buildings in which their processes were done.

Soon, I saw ahead of me on the right of the road a
great red brick building, three storeys high and of im-
mense length and breadth. Other buildings stretched
away behind it, with smoking chimneys. The road
was black with crowds going in at the gates. The trolley-cars were in their rush-hour service, bringing people to work: the morning flood was running. To the
left of the mill-road was a hill, partly sunburnt grass,

4

partly built upon.   To the right of it, behind the mill-
buildings, was the shallow valley of the Nepperhan,
in which one could distinguish the water-course.   Beyond this, to the eastward, there was quiet, untouched
country again, with seemingly virgin woodland, growing maple, with undergrowths of sumach.

When I last saw this place the building was un-
changed in its outward aspect, but it seemed to have
shrunk to half its size.   When I first saw it early in that
September morning more than forty-five years ago, it
seemed vast.   Often in the months which followed, it
seemed vast.   Certainly, when I first had to do with it,
I had never been associated with any building so big.
It loomed up above the road, like a gigantic ship taking in passengers at a dockside.   As I drew nearer, I
heard the enormous murmur of its engines, and saw a
general quickening in the steps of those entering.   It
was now almost seven o'clock.

My friend shewed me where I was to wait.   He
passed on into the building.   I was in a little room
near an office at the gate.   About a dozen people were
there, mostly women of about twenty or twenty-five;
there were two men, one of them a fairly tough-looking
man who looked as though he had been a ship's fire-
man, as indeed he had been.   In a moment or two,
the great seven o'clock whistle blew, and an elderly
Scots engineer shut the gates on those who were late.
Some had run it too fine and were shut out.   As the
whistle started, the noise of the engines which had

been a steady booming murmur rose up into a clanging roar; the day's work had begun.

Almost at once the floor-bosses began to interview
the applicants. It seems to me now, that Johnny was
wrong about the depression. Things had been quiet
for some months, perhaps; they were now improving,
and hands were being taken on. I suppose I was the
youngest there; I know that I was the last dealt with.
I remember that the one questioned before me was a
young woman, who had been there before as a setter.
The floor-boss said. "You had a good job here. Why
did you throw it in?"

"I had a mistake to fix. I guess I was mad. I
wouldn't fix it."

"It was your mistake, you'd ought to have fixed it."

"I guess I was mad."

"Now you want to come back?"

"Yes."

"All right. But suppose you make another mistake?"

"I guess I'll fix it."

This was enough; a skilled setter was needed; she
was told to go on up.

My turn came next. A man said: "You're the boy
Billy mentioned? You want to come here? Your
name's John? You can start in right away. George,
take this lad up to Tommy's will you?"

I went out of the office with George, crossed the
track, went up the wooden steps and through some big

6

green doors into a deafening, roaring, clanging clack in which one had to shout to make oneself heard. We were on the lower weaving-floor, where I suppose more than a hundred power-looms were in full work. All the floor on each side of the gangway was filled with looms, nearly all in action. The shuttles were stabbing and clacking, the belts were humming, the swords were coming back with a bang, and the appalling ceiling of advancing spools shook and jerked overhead. The noise was like nothing that I had ever heard. The air was already filled with wool-dust, and sweepers were moving along the gangway with their great brooms to sweep away the coloured dust. From the constant sweeping away of the wool-dust (if not from the lanoline) the floors of all the gangways were very slippery. Having learned this in my first minute, I had not to be reminded later. A good many electric lights were burning, for the weavers, men and women, needed all the light they could get. We went through part of this floor, then up more stairs, to a floor where the noise was even greater; then up more stairs, to a floor where the noise changed suddenly to something much less but quicker in its tempo. The weaving floors had been shouting, in the main

Terack. Terack. Crash. BANG.

Here the machines were only repeating Terack, as a couple of hundred young women twitched threads of wool over threading-hooks. Going through this room, George led me into a vast room stretching on into a northern darkness. In the south-eastern quarter of this room some men were working machines with the skill and speed of machines, while others supplied their labour. Men were passing to and fro with racks and trucks of peculiar makes, all laden with spools of wool. On the western side of the room there was a great office with cupboards stuffed with thousands of coloured, varnished carpet-designs, any one of which might be ordered at any minute. The machines at which the men were working made a good deal of noise, their belts hummed and the great knives within them clashed as the men pressed the pedals. George handed me over to Tommy and sped away to his own work on a lower floor. Tommy said he was glad I'd come, for Charlie was going at the end of the day. He handed me over to Charlie, who had just one day in which to teach me his mystery.

Charlie was much liked throughout that floor. He was a very quiet, clever, deeply religious, young American, singularly thoughtful and good, and with much merriment. He said that he was going to work in the dyeing rooms after that day. Later, I found that the dyeing-room jobs were much sought after, being very highly paid. They had disadvantages. In some of them, the dyes coloured the hands of the workers, so that they were subdued to what they worked in. It was a daily experience there to meet men with green, bright yellow or purple hands and arms. They themselves did not mind; they were proud of the mark; it shewed the world that they were in the dyeing rooms, earning big money; but it was said that women shrank from them. In some of the processes, steam was much used; I believe that it always was much used in the fixing of the colours. I only once entered the dyeing rooms; it was there that I last saw Charlie. I found the place thick with steam and very hot and clammy. This was the main disadvantage; but the dyers always said that they became used to it after the first few days and that it had no ill effects.

I learned from Charlie the rudiments of the work he did; it was simple enough, but it needed close attention, a quick eye, and care.

I need only say here, that the strips of carpet came down from the setting-rooms to our section as wool of different colours tightly wrapped round wooden spools of varying lengths, some of them more than a yard long, most of them (at a guess) about two feet six inches long, and some of them only covered with wool for five-eighths of their length. These spools were arranged in order in sets of ten. Usually, I suppose, about 200 spools made a length of carpet. When they came down, they were sometimes put into store, sometimes ordered at once to some particular loom on the weaving-floor. If they were to be woven-off at once, they were loaded into racks, in divisions of ten spools, and taken to the threading or tinning-room to be threaded. A girl would take each spool in order, fix to it a rather heavy metal frame bearing on it a row of nearly two hundred little tin tubes, and would then work a mechanical threading-hook so that each line of wool on the spool was pulled through one of the tin tubes. When all the spools were threaded or, as we usually called it, tinned, the sett of spools was dragged into our section, to the cutters, who combed and evenly cut the ends of wool protruding from the tubes.

The cutting-machines were sufficiently terrible. Each was run by one man, who took out each spool from the sett allotted to him, combed it with a swift tug on a metal comb fixed upon his cutter, dropped the spool-ends into the slots prepared, thrust his right foot to the pedal, and released the great knife, which rushed out horizontally towards him and sliced off the ragged ends of the wool. There were always two, usually three and sometimes four cutters working. Their skill and speed were wonderful. I saw them every day and never ceased to wonder at the precision and delicacy of their movements. Each spool had to be lifted delicately, because careless handling might unthread some tufts of wool from the tin tubes, each had to be combed delicately yet surely before going under the knife, and care had to be taken, not to expose too much wool to the blade. The dropping of the spool into the slots had to be accurate and sure, for if the knife went through the tubes there was trouble. After cutting, the spool had to be replaced in the rack accurately and delicately. When the mill was busy and the looms were crying out for setts, the cutters were at their task all day long, cutting, as I judge, one spool in every seven seconds. Some very big spools took longer; the little, three-quarter spools, took less. The floor near the cutters was worn into deep, polished grooves by their sliding feet. They warned me to be very careful of the combs on their cutters. These were sharp and varied according to the nature of the wool in use, but were all likely to give a nasty scratch which would fester. The wool sliced off by the knives fell into boxes below the machine. A man collected these clippings several times a day, and a use was found for them; they made a special kind of mat with them. Another man examined the cuttings several times a day, to make sure that they were not too long. The cutters were all piece-workers.

It was after the cutters had trimmed-off and replaced the spools that Charlie's work began. It was necessary to make sure that the outer tin tubes in each metal frame were not unduly pushed outwards or inwards. If they were bent in either way, they made the edge of the woven carpet uneven, "they made a bad selvage." To make sure that the outer tubes were not improperly bent, we straightened them with a little metal tool. It had a boxwood handle like a bradawl and a slightly curving metal blade, not very sharp, about an inch broad. I have never seen any tool in the least like it. It was called a "tin-opener." It was admirable for the work it did; I suppose it had been made in the mills' workshops for the purpose it served. When the tin tubes had been straightened, the anxious part of our work began. We had to make sure, that each one of each ten spools was in its right place, and that each ten was arranged in the proper order in the rack.

Each spool was coloured on its ends; each set of ten was arranged in the same order. 1. Red. 2. White. 3. Blue. 4. Orange. 5. Drab. 6. Yellow. 7. Green. 8. Brown. 9. Scarlet. 10. Black.

When the spools were new and the colours bright it was easy to see that they were in their proper order. When they were not so new, when the colours were dimmed, a little carelessness from someone might mistake the red for the scarlet, or the orange for either, or for the yellow. Some of the brown spools, when dirty, passed for black, and the green spools, when faded, passed for drab. We had to look out for these transpositions, to make sure that they had not been made. This needed a special sense, which developed very swiftly.

Then we had to make sure, that the tens were in their proper order; sometimes they were reversed, or worse. This needed an adaptation of that special sense. If we were in doubt, we went to the office for the design of the carpet, and from this made certain that the order of each ten was right. We had also to be sure, that no single line of wool had come to be unthreaded from its tube. If we found such a line, we threaded it by means of a tiny hook of wire, which we carried for the purpose.

If we found any spool-end or metal-frame loose, we had to take it to be doctored by two young craftsmen who worked at a table against our southern wall.

When we were sure that the sett was in order, we initialled the card fixed upon it and dragged the rack to the elevator nearest to the loom to which it had to go.

The elevator-man in my section was a fine young fellow named Perce. His main interest in life was pugilism. He welcomed me that first morning as a man likely to be able to tell him about the best English boxers, and perhaps give him light on the great question, would Peter Maher beat Bob Fitzsimmons. I did not think that he would, nor did he, but this led to the question, whether Sharkey would beat Fitzsimmons, or whether Joe Choynski could. At intervals we raised these topics throughout the day. Near the elevator worked by Perce there was a water-point with a dipper, for those who thirsted. It was a hot, fine, New York September, very hot indeed for so late in the season. I remember clearly the delight of that abundant clear cold water. I do not know where the water came from, perhaps from those beautiful Croton lakes which I had seen that spring. "Water is the best thing" someone said. To anyone who has been on short allowance of water in a hot climate abundant cool water will seem the best of all things. All through my time there, I felt the benefit of that excellent water, so abundant and so good.

Work went on until twelve, when the whistle blew and power suddenly ceased to work the machines, which died down into stillness. Most of those who lived near by went home to lunch; the rest found snug nooks and lunched at ease about the sections. After about twenty minutes, groups of people drifted through the section and paused on their way for a little chaff. The office-workers had some round flat metal paper-weights. With these, they began a game of curling on the floor. We joined in this. For some weeks, it was a favourite amusement during the lunch interval; many, who did not play, came in to watch.

At a minute or two before a quarter to one, the power began to set the belts in movement. The piece-workers started their machines as soon as they had power enough; usually they got in an extra minute, I think, before the lunch hour was over. With an extra minute before seven in the morning, and this extra minute at noon they may have won twelve minutes from the company during an average week. As the whistle blew, the work began again at full strength. Probably, everybody was ready to begin at the very instant of the whistle.

Work went on until six in the evening. At about a minute before six the cutters stopped cutting, passed a handful of wool-clip over their blades, and whisked

14

some of the fluff from their persons. There was a
general slackening up and preparing to go, though
this was often checked by authority. Still, when the
whistle blew nearly everybody was ready to go; the
machines stopped, the looms were no longer banging.
At the first blast of the whistle there was a rush to the
stairs and between five and six thousand men and
women made for home. At the trolley terminus, perhaps half a dozen trolley-cars waited for those with a
long journey before them. Most of the people walked.
I walked back with a man who talked to me very
seriously about the mill. "You are in the mill, now,"
he said. "These people are always on the look-out
for talent. If you shew that you are interested and
keen, they'll give you every chance. There are lots
of men on each floor who have suggested improve-
ments, or invented processes and are reaping the benefit. There's one man, who improved one of the looms;
he got twenty thousand dollars for it. There is no
place in the whole mill that is not open to you if you
care to go for it. It would be a proud thing, to start
as you do and perhaps in ten or fifteen years become
one of the managers. It's all in your own hands; in
ten or fifteen years you might be that; don't you think
you'd be proud? But you'll have to shew them that
you mean business; you'll have to work; and out of
business you'll have to be steady. They have ways
of knowing how their people behave after hours.
There was one of the floor-bosses in the weaving-rooms

who went into a saloon for a glass of beer; they knew
about it somehow and asked him how about it? You'll
not find any of the likely men here ever entering a
saloon, and believe me, they find their reward for it.
They are made to feel that they're respected for it, and
shoved forward. So, think of this. It's all in your
own hands, and there's no position on the pay-roll that
you might not win to, if you've a mind for it."

I supped at the Restaurant; then went to my lodging to think over these words and the day's experience.
For some years, at intervals, whenever life was not
pressing too hard and making me too tired at the end
of a day, I had practised the getting of tranquillity
before going to sleep. I cannot now recollect how
this habit had begun; but I had found the benefit of
emptying the mind of worry, whenever I turned in to
my hammock on the *Conway*. Sometimes, I had repeated the process in the early morning before
turning out, so as to start the day with a quiet mind.
The process was very simple. I read a page of some
thoughtful prose, then, shutting my eyes, I repeated
to myself a couple of poems, and then sang to myself
with a mental voice, one, two, three or even four songs.
Usually, before I reached the fourth, I had attained
a mental quiet, in which I could sort out the experience of the day, annul its trouble as illusion and see
its good as jolly. It seems to me, on looking back,
that I began this habit on the *Conway* at a time when
I was very much perplexed by the troubles which

16

follow promotion, "the sweets of office" as they are called. Often enough, I did not attempt the process; sometimes, it did not work; but when it did work, it made me master of the day.

For some few weeks in New York I had found this way of quiet very helpful. When I went to bed at Yonkers that night, I got into my mood of quiet, and went over the events of the day and the prospects which opened before me. I was young, but I had learned that the world on one side of a fence is a pretty tough joint of snatch and grab driven by a callousness of greed which the world on the other side of the fence calls by very different names. I had no doubt whatever that this "job which I had struck," for that was the phrase in use, was by much the best job which I had so far met with; the liberty was greater, the pay incredibly much better, and the work infinitely lighter. I know that I was very happy at the results of the day; but I wondered whether I should be good enough to be kept on. Should I be able "to hold-down the job" as it was called. I feared that I might not be able enough in some way. Besides, I was English, and this was America; if the judgment of Johnny were right, if the country really were going through a crisis, then, surely, the Englishman would be sacked so as to give the native American a chance; if not, then I might expect trouble from the natives, "that I was taking the bread from an American's mouth." These thoughts were much in my mind. On the other hand, I knew that I was industrious, that I was trained to work hard, and needed no supervision to keep me at my task. My present work called for industry and good sight; both of which I had in abundance. Still, it seemed almost too much to expect that a job of the sort would long be mine; I could only hope it might be.

On trying to sleep, I was roused by the patter of tiny feet and the nibble of minute mouths. The light shewed me that the room swarmed with cockroaches, which had crept out of the crannies and were every-where. The chinks in the plaster shewed their little heads flairing the prospect; some of the creatures had come on to my bed and nibbled at my toes. I had been in a ship multitudinously infested with these things and had no particular horror of them. They were a nuisance, for they kept me awake, but nothing like such a nuisance as mosquitoes. They were noth-ing to the infestations in a certain room of frightful memory in New York, where four different kinds of vampire had attacked me simultaneously. The main bother was, that the room had been engaged for me for one week, and I could not afford to take another. "Grin and bear it" is the word for youth. What are a few cockroaches to the amazing exquisite bliss of having all-night-in? I was free to lie in bed till nearly six next morning. To one who had been at watch and watch and gone short of sleep for days and nights together, this liberty of rest was in itself a joy diffi-cult to put into words. I found it possible to keep the cockroaches from touching me; after all, their nibbles were only experimental; they never succeeded in biting through. I had learned two of the blessings of life, abundant water, abundant sleep; I slept in peace.

On the second morning, the honey-coloured waiter at the Restaurant remembered me and greeted me with a smile. "You only want coffee again dis morning?" he asked. "You set right here." However, I wanted more than coffee, and was advised to try a plate of bucks, with maple syrup; when made, as those were made, by a negro cook, these things are great delicacies. It was still, exquisite blue September weather; the lovely River with her cliffs lay just down the road. I set out from the Square after breakfast feeling that I trod an enchanted world of beauty and strangeness. The avenues along which I walked were well planted with trees, now turning colour. Hundreds of people were going in my direction; one or two who knew me, called out greeting to me; their friendliness was very gracious, for I was a stranger, a foreigner, still expecting the half-brick from behind a tree. It was exhilarating to be going with all those hundreds, to be a part of so great a will to work. A couple of men joined me, and we walked on together.

When we were about 500 yards from the mill, at a cross-roads, I saw an old woman standing looking towards our group as we advanced. She had something of a haggard lost look. She came towards us with uncertain steps and peered into our faces. One of the men with me, said "No; none of us, Mother, but he'll be around later, sure to." She made a noise in her throat and moved away to look into the faces of others. "She's looking for her son" my companion said, "he marched away by this road in the Civil War, going to New York. She generally comes out to look for him when people are going to work."

"Was the son killed, then?"

"I guess so. Anyways, he didn't come back. Lots were lost in the War and nobody knew what had happened to them."

I saw that poor woman many hundreds of times still looking for the son who had gone more than thirty years before. This was the first time that I was brought face to face with the unending, never-to-be-comforted sorrow which comes with war, that accursed abomination with which soldiers, statesmen and all with debased views of life afflict mankind.

My first days in the new way of life were anxious, but exciting and delightful. They were anxious, because I was doubtful whether I could keep the job, and because I still expected some of the hazing to which new-comers anywhere are usually subject; they were exciting, because the experience was big, and new; they were delightful because I found the work easy and the people welcoming. They mocked me a little for my "English accent" and for one or two ways which they thought odd; they made good-humoured

remarks such as "Why do you call your little island
Great? Gee, you can't hardly see it on the map."
Otherwise, they were all friendly and put me at my
ease at once. Within a few days, they let me know,
that I was approved; one of them told me that he had
heard the boss say, that the new lad whom Billy sent
was a good one; and another said, that he had heard
my section-boss say "That he liked that new lad, but
there was one thing he couldn't understand about
him; he went on working without being told; he didn't
have to be watched. Gee, I don't understand it."
All men work and hope for praise of some sort, this
was my first praise; it came at a time when I deeply
needed it and it gave me great joy. I knew, now,
that I could hold down the job, and that the men accepted me. I was one of the crew; they would offer
me fruit from their lunches and share similar goods
from me; and at first they daily asked me for or offered
me chews of the very strong black hairy chewing tobacco, which I think few seamen could have managed
without qualms, but which they took with relish.
They mocked me a little for not chewing. "When
you chew, you know you're dealing with tobacco;
you're not just filling your mouth with a lot of smoke."
But in my past I had seen many boys trying to learn
to chew, and had watched many discover beyond doubt
that they were dealing with tobacco, and praying for
kindly death.

I suppose that in a week I had learned all the details

of my work, had come to know what to look for, what to guard against, and some of the mistakes (made by others) which we could discover and set right before harm was done. In this last part of the work, we had less thought of our employers than of our fellow workers, whose jobs I do not doubt we sometimes saved to them. I know that in the first six months of my stay there, the work became more exacting; we were shewn, that we had to watch for many more things than Charlie had had to watch. I can say that no error of any serious sort got by me while I was doing that work. The only difficulty was the handling of the spool-racks. These were often very heavy and demanded a knack, which did not come to me for the first few days.

The racks ran upon four small wheels. They stood about seven feet, they had a length of eight or nine feet, and a breadth of about thirty inches. When filled with spools of certain sorts, for the broader carpet-strips, which we called "yard-wides," they bristled at both sides, with protruding spool-ends and metal-clips. The setts of yard-wides usually contained more spools than other setts; they filled the racks from top to bottom. When pulling a rack full of yard-wide spools towards the elevators, it was often difficult to guide. You took the rack by its forward end and pulled it gently towards you, as you backed in the required direction. Often the gangway was not very broad, for there might be rows of racks on both sides of it.   If the wheels of the rack were even a little clogged with wool-dust which had caught in the grease there, one or other of them would stick and the steering would go wrong.   The vessel would yaw or take a sheer.   Like a ship taking a sheer, a rack on that ever slippery floor might take charge and go with a wallop into some other sett and do much damage to both. The protruding clips caught or broke, and an hour's extra work might follow.   After watching the cutters (who were admirably skilled in the handling of setts), and having some narrow squeaks, I got the hang of them.   I could coax even a stubborn mule of a rack from between two others almost hooking into it.   I could even coax it backwards in between two others, with only an inch or two of clearance on each side. Now and then, we had to deal with a really difficult rack, a brute that would neither stay nor wear.   Such an one might take four men to take down the gangway and load into the elevator.

Among the many national prejudices and beliefs which had been impressed upon me in my upbringing few escaped a jolt of some sort in those first days. I remember a man asking:—

"Say, did you ever see the Queen?"

"No, never."

Here my questioner asked, if a fantastic absurd tale about her were true?   It was a question which had been put to me almost daily for the last five months; and so crazy as to take away the breath.

"True? No, of course it isn't true."

"I guess it is true; everybody says so here. I guess you may not be allowed to say it in your old country."

"But I never heard such rubbish in my life. If you would spend a day in England you would know that it couldn't be true." Indeed, the suggestion was of the very maddest, incongruous absurdity. My questioner shook his head. "Too many people say so" he said, "I guess you'll have a revolution in England when she dies. The Prince of Wales won't ever be King?"

"Of course he will; there won't be a revolution."

"Everybody says so here. What d'you want a King or Queen for anyway?"

"To be head of the State."

"You got a head of the state in your Prime Minister, haven't you?"

"Yes, but he depends on a vote of the people; the Sovereign is a permanent head, to whom everybody looks up."

"Could she cut off the Prime Minister's head, if he got anyways gay?"

"No, of course she couldn't."

"Well, how's she the permanent head, then?"

"She IS. But the laws settle matters of punishing."

"Then the law's the permanent head?"

"No; the law is the Sovereign's will."

"Well, why can't she cut off the Prime Minister's head, then?"

"Because the Prime Minister leads Parliament, and Parliament would want a say in the matter."

He shook his head again. "It seems all mixed up to me," he said. "You've got all this kennel of dogs and each has to do the other's barking, it seems to me." I assured him that perhaps I had not described it too clearly, but that it worked out all right; he was not persuaded. Other men from time to time came to ask me about the Queen: if the fantastic tale were true. I denied it vigorously and began to wonder if the question were put as a traditional way of ragging an Englishman. A minute's thought shewed me, that they had no wish to annoy me; they didn't mind me in spite of my "English accent"; they had heard a remarkable tale, and asked, if it were true. I could not imagine how the tale had started; it puzzled me for years. It was only a few months ago that a newspaper printed something which gave me the clue to the mistake which set the absurd fable forth.

Probably, the life of the fable was not very long. In the years before the Diamond Jubilee, the English Queen was more talked-of than any other person in the world. When I revisited the United States twenty years later all memory of the tale had passed away.

It was strange, perplexing, vexing and very good for me to be in a community which held opinions so new to me. I had not thought it possible, that anyone could without danger hold any opinions other than those which had been given to me as final truth.

Could it really be, that a great nation could for one moment suppose that anything English could be anything but perfect? Was not our record the story of one long glorious triumph? It was true that we had lost the battle of Senlac, but that was because most of our army had been killed a few days before somewhere; and anyhow, we absorbed the Normans after it.

"Saxon and Norman and Dane are we."

But here I was in a nation which did not seem to set much store by us, no great, particular store. Like most English boys of that time, I was almost completely ignorant of American history. I knew a few facts and dates about Virginia, Captain John Smith, Sir Walter Raleigh, tobacco, the potato, the Pilgrim Fathers and George Washington and his axe. I knew nothing whatever about the War of Independence, not much about the War of 1812, and very little about the War of the Secession. I think that I had a contented belief, that America had once been English, that she had chosen to break away, and must ever since have been suffering from the consequences. I now found that I was living with men to whom American History was a matter of extraordinary pride, and that this history shewed an England very different from the one in my heart. I learned, in fact, that in great questions there are two sides.

"Though Law be made for half of the world, the breaker of Law has half." The shock to myself was profound, cruel and full of anguish. For a few days,

26

probably, I trembled for America; then I said to myself "Lookers-on see most of the game; let me try to
get this point of view. Is the England that they describe the real England, or have they been taught a
lot of rubbish?" I recognized that all the men in my
section were men of English stock; all had English
names, though all except myself were Americans born.
All were extraordinarily nice to me; they knew that
I couldn't help being English; it wasn't my fault; and
all, without exception, spoke of England as "the old
country," a phrase possibly less frequent in America
today, but singularly grateful to an exile's ear. But
there they were maintaining, that their forefathers had
beaten the English armies or captured them, captured
English ships, destroyed an English fleet (on Lake
Erie), established a great principle, "No taxation without representation"; and that only two Kings in our
history mattered to them; Charles the First, because
men like the Pilgrim Fathers had rebelled against him,
and George the Third because they had won their
freedom from him. The depth, width and emptiness
of my ignorance of American history kept me from
all reply. My mind received jolt after jolt. Other
jolts were to follow very swiftly, and each came with
a cruel certainty upon a prejudice based upon an ignorance.

The teaching of Irish history had been much neglected among those trained for the Merchant Service
in my youth. I think that it had been summed up in

one sentence running like this. "The history of Ireland in past, and even in present times, makes but melancholy reading." In some book I had seen a list of ancient Irish kings, most of whom had been murdered or killed in battle; I had been impressed by this list, and had thought that it did make melancholy reading. Apart from this I knew nothing about Ireland, except that I had heard odd remarks about crime in Ireland, shooting of landlords, evictions, agitations, etc. I had not read of these things; I had but heard people speak of them, usually with indignation, that the Irish could not accept the blessings of English rule. I had met a good many Irish; there were always some first rate specimens on the *Conway* in my day; they had not found anything wrong with us. Now I met with some of a very different camp.

In the mill, in sections with which mine had sometimes much to do, were three Irishmen, from each of whom I soon began to learn; two, who were Roman Catholics, shewed me that they looked upon the English as heretics, with a kind of pity and horror mixed, as though "mouldy old Prots," which was their word for Anglicans, really shewed by their dread of holy water that they were mad dogs dangerous to the world. The third shewed to me with what fanatical passion of hatred the Irish cause is sometimes followed. He was a middle-aged man, in whom for certainly thirty years every faculty of intellect and feeling had been driven by hatred of England. He never spoke save against us; he never read save to find something to wrest to our damnation. The intensity of his loathing was something for which I was utterly unprepared. The extent of his knowledge of recent history gave me no defence against him. At first I hated him bitterly, and all the more because he was so friendly to myself; however, we became friends.

I know, that all through my first month in the mill, I was extremely happy. I had been able to settle down with my fellows; I had held the job, I could do it well, and heard indirect praise of myself. Then it brought with it enormous advantages, for which I had longed unavailingly for years.

After a week in the cockroach room, I heard of, and went to, a room in a neat little white frame house close to the woods outside the town. Here I settled myself. Its only disadvantage was that it was a longish way from the Restaurant where I took my meals, so that I had about a mile and a half added to my daily walking.

I now began to take stock of the situation, and to wonder whether I could make this mill my life's work, and rise, as my friend had suggested, section by section, floor by floor, to profitable heights.

Deep within myself was a longing to be a writer; but this longing was very deeply buried, under the more immediate longing to read and read, and not to be so ignorant. I wanted to know all that men had thought and done. Years before, on the *Con-*

way, I had seen in Mr. Foxley's cabin on the lower deck, an engraving of Ulysses passing the Sirens, with the lines

"Approach, thy soul shall into raptures rise,
Approach, and learn new wisdom from the wise."

I wanted my soul to have a chance to rise into raptures, and I longed to learn new wisdom and old, too. If I could do that, I thought, then, possibly, some day, even I might be able to write something, some sort of a story, perhaps. My friends said that only clever people could hope to make a living by writing, that it was like pugilism, "Many are called but few are chosen," and that those not chosen lived in garrets, and took drugs till they went raving mad and died and were buried by the parish. This seemed to me true. It was most unlikely that I should ever be able to write anything which anyone would print or pay me for; yet deep within me writing lured me, something urged me to read and read. It did not tell me what to read, and I did not know; but one of the joys of my job was that it gave me time to read, and that was a joy past telling. Of course, I knew, that there might come a depression, when hands would be turned off, and that then I, as a foreigner and a new-comer should be one of the first sent away. Well, the thought of a depression was not new to me. Seamen suffered from depressions. I had seen shipping offices in three or four ports crowded with seamen "outward-bound"

as we called it, each with a handful of excellent dis-
charges, yet all unable to get a ship. It had seemed
to me likely that in a new land like America, a farm-
hand would be sure of work all the year round. I had
learned that that was not so. Farmers often sacked
their men when the harvest was in, keeping perhaps
only one man through the winter to do the milking;
the rest might wander. Depressions seemed to me a
part of life, to be expected like snowstorms or frosts
or fogs. I must expect depressions. Until one struck
me, I judged I would stay where I was if the people
would keep me.

When I compared the work with what I had already
done, it had overwhelming advantages. The drawbacks were of course considerable. All the work was
done indoors, in air always somewhat fluffy with float-
ing wool-dust (on the weaving-floors thick with it).
After the open air of the sea and the farm this was a
hardship, since I have ever loved clean air. Still, so
far, it was hot autumn weather and the great windows
were still mostly open. Then, compared with work
on a farm, it lacked the exhilarating variety of the
many morning and evening chores, and the main task,
so different from them, at which one sang with one's
fellows, enjoying every moment. My farm work had
been done in spring and early summer; it had been
wholly delightful; but my friends told me, that I
should have found it a different thing in the winter.
"All you'd be doing then would be shovelling the

snow to make a way to the cowshed, and getting frost-bitten while you do it, then milking the cows with your forehead in a cow's wet flank, and her tail whacking you across the face, and then getting pneumonia as you bring the milk in." Still, I thought of the life as I had known it, and regretted the exquisite days, the poultry, the cattle, the magnificent ploughing-oxen, and the exhilaration of the earth. Compared with the life at sea the mill life lacked the companionship of the sky and the continual interest of the weather. Memorable beauty companions the sailor. I longed for morning watches in the tropics, or sunsets in the second dog watch. I longed also for the sight of ships and the interest of rigging. I missed the personal jobs which fall even to boys at sea. Sometimes even a boy will be trusted to do a neat little job in seamanship, such as pointing a rope, making a mat of some kind, putting a new becket, with Matthew Walkers, on a bucket, or in his spare time beginning a wonderful pair of shackles, such as no other chest could boast. Then, I missed very much, the link of the ship; no man can fail to feel for a ship as for a living thing, and though the affection can be very well disguised, it is there, she is a living thing, sometimes almost a divine thing, who demands and receives service.

Then, she is always a beautiful thing, usually, in my time, a superlatively lovely thing, exquisite to see; no man could call the mill good-looking. But when I

had mourned for these good things, I reflected, that
on the farm I had always risen at four in the morning,
and had never finished the evening chores before eight
at night, and that though there had been intervals for
the abundant and welcome meals, I had worked hard
for fifteen hours in each day, and had had no leisure
save between the chores on Sundays. At sea, one had
been always at watch and watch, with the certainty of
having to work in a watch below if there were trouble
even of a lesser sort. Any leisure used for study was
taken from necessary sleep, and then with every con-
ceivable disadvantage which the public life of the sea
entails. Then, at sea, in addition to the hardness of
the work at all times and the hardships of cold and
wet, one suffered from the semi-starvation of the lime-
juicer's allowance, which was much the kind of food
given to the ordinary dog, but markedly worse than
that given to the hound. The hound has boiled
horse. God knows what it was that the seamen had.
Then, I had seen the sea close to, for some years. I
had known first-rate seamen ruined by a moment's
miscalculation, some running of a light too fine, some
failure to read the evidence in fog or blind weather,
just one error, perhaps, after twenty years of careful
triumph. After that, what was their chance of getting command again? And what was command? I
had heard seamen ask it, saying that it was responsibility of an exacting kind, which might be ended
without compensation at an employer's whim at any

moment. They said that it brought with it the too frequent absence from home, "Almost no home life," for the privilege of taking another man's ship, perhaps into hell and back. How many sea captains had spoken thus in my hearing, saying, "You young fellows, get out of it, before the life gets you; a man who would go to sea for pleasure would go to hell for pastime." Well, even so, men did go to sea for pleasure; it was a grand life, no-one could deny that; but if you wanted to read and read, it was the wrong life.

I never heard that any of my fellows in the mill belonged to any Union. We were all well content with our lot. In all my time there I heard no serious complaint against the management or the conditions of service. We were all made to feel that if we wished to work we should get on. We knew that we were getting a square deal; in return we gave our best. That best was very good indeed. I know not what caused the rush, whether an improvement in business as a whole, or some few big special orders. Certainly, soon after my coming there we had a week or two in which we were rushing all day long. The racks of setts poured out from the storage-bins into the tinning-room; they filled all the gangways there; they were dragged to the cutters as fast as they could be threaded; all the knives were manned and the cutters worked as never before. There were, if I remember rightly, four knives at work together, cutting in all about eleven setts in the hour. It was not possible for two

tin-openers to pass eleven setts in the hour. In each
sett some four hundred little tin tubes had to be
straightened or seen to be straight and after that the
orders of the spools and the tens had to be verified. A
third tin-opener came on to the task; sometimes also
a part-time fourth; even so we were put to our trumps
to keep the setts from blocking the gangways. We
were at it at a breathless rush all day long. Sometimes we felt that the setts were gaining on us, sometimes we seemed to win a little ahead.

At sea and elsewhere I had known great rushes of
work which had somehow to be done. At sea, the
urging force was necessity; if such and such things
were not done in time there would be disaster and
an all-hands-job. On a farm the method used was
bribery. "Sons, get this job done, and you shall all
have some apple-jack and chicken-pot-pie for supper."
In the mill we were just told to hustle and we hustled
because we knew that we were squarely dealt with
and must deal squarely in return. Not one man failed
to do his utmost, though all knew that if we slacked
we might make extraordinarily profitable overtime.
We put our backs into the job and got it done without
any overtime. We had a few words of praise for our
hard work and some little "raises" in pay as a reward.
I have to this day the memory of the exhilaration of
the rush. We pitted ourselves against the task and
beat it.

When I had settled down to the routine of the mill

I did as my fellows did. I found that the best foot-gear for the mill were somebody's excellent dollar shoes. They cost exactly one dollar the pair; if worn daily they lasted for one month of thirty days. If they were rested and often changed they lasted more than twice as long. If I bought three pairs at once the three would last for seven months at least. Having fended for myself in these ways from an early age, I polished my shoes for myself; but sometimes followed the custom of the country, sat in the brass chair at the square corner, and had a five-cent shine.

Men have often said that America is a costly country. All countries have costly shops and quarters but, in nearly all, those who know where to go can live well and very cheaply. America was and is a land of extraordinary abundance and cheapness, too. Clothes were very cheap and good. In the mill the summer day and the winter steam-heat made it impossible to wear a coat while at work. The work was not destructive of clothes; it was dry and did not soil what one wore. At first I found that little metal clips on the ends of wool-spools were apt to catch in clothes, especially at elbows and knees, and give little characteristic triangular tears. I soon learned to look out for these. In any case, I was able to mend such tears for myself. I needed only a few cheap clothes for work-days, and some rather better things for Sundays. Like the other mill-hands, I bought these at a big clothing store near the Square. Generally, Americans wear light clothing, winter and summer, their houses being so well warmed; their only winter addition is the overcoat for out of doors.   The good dark Sunday suits in the store cost about two dollars fifty.   New York, even, then, was the centre of an enormous, highly skilled trade in cheap, mass-produced, ready-made and excellent clothing, which went all over the United States.

I took my laundry each week to one or other of the Chinese laundries.

The laundries were very much alike; a small reception room near the street, with a counter across it, and shelves bearing neat packets of washing on the wall behind the counter.   Further inside, one usually saw, either the steam of the work, or some sign of the laundryman's ease.   Sometimes, there were bunks to be seen, containing resting Chinamen, often smoking strange pipes, which I took to be opium pipes.   Always, the outer windows of the shops were covered with fine wire-mesh.   As one Chinaman said to me. "Mellican boy, he flingee Tone."   The Chinese were all men; it was said that no Chinese women were allowed to land.   They all worked very hard and saved money; all went home to China, or were shipped home, dead, in their coffins.   All wore Chinese costume, which seemed to suit every kind of weather, and always looked delightful.   All had a charm of manner which I found irresistible; all had such a look of cleverness, of ancient culture and of wisdom; all were such good workmen, so courteous and so merry. I never called for my packet of laundry without a little talk with whatever Chinaman was on duty; and never failed to think "This is the East, the wise East, whose missionaries ought to be in every country in Europe; but they are too truly polite to try to teach anyone."

However, my American friends told me that these Chinamen were full of feud among themselves, and that in their feuds some terrible fellows, known as "high-binders," knocked their enemies on the head with sand-bags; and that anyway a Chink would gamble his grandfather's pigtail at fan-tan. "Gee, these Chinks, they're up to anything."

Since then, I have come to feel that every nation pretty much will be up to anything if given the chance of making something by it. I still think that the East dresses better and has more winning manners and is more industrious, and has a deeper root in traditional wisdom than our feverish West.

I have continued to long for missionaries from the East, to give us a tranquillity, but have come to think it more likely that western barbarism may engulf even what remains of Eastern tranquillity, and bring back Dark Ages to the world, so that man may start again.

From the first, I lived in what my fellows called the European system, hiring a bedroom and getting my meals at the Restaurant. Most of my fellows lived at home, or in boarding-houses. I had a feeling that they thought the European system something dark and feudal, with a guilty kind of splendour about it; just a touch of the wicked lord. When I revisited Yonkers after many years, I sought for the Restaurant in vain; even in the South I have never known such bucks; and my friend, the honey-coloured negro waiter, where was he?

Though my first beginnings of mill-life were delightful to me, the discovery of the country near me was rapture. On my first Sunday I found myself saying "I have the entire day, wholly to myself." I had never before been able to say this. It was glorious, fair, sunny September weather, with the hard, clear, rapturous New York light and that exhilaration in the air which impels all New Yorkers to do twice man's normal work on half the food and a third of the sleep. I went down to the Restaurant to breakfast, and then at once to the River, to gaze at the noble line of cliffs, the marvellous water and the cat-boats heading away towards the Tappan Zee. I had never looked on anything more beautiful. I walked up the River till I found a man who had boats to let; I took a boat and rowed across, made fast under the cliffs and went exploring. To my amazement I found the Jersey shore almost untouched by man; no one seemed to have trodden those screes or broken through the scrub. I found a place by which I could scramble to the cliff-top; there I found what seemed to be primitive woodland, stretching away into Jersey. I walked for a while inland, till I came to a track and a little farm; it might

have been hard to find anything lonelier in Wisconsin,
and this was a dozen miles from New York City. I
saw no one, heard no one. If there were people at
the farm, they may have been asleep. I walked back
to the cliff-top, and gazed long at the River, which
from that side presents a gentle prospect, Eve-like and
gracious, compared with the cliffs on which I stood.
It seemed to me that no one could be long unhappy
beside a place so beautiful. "Whatever happens," I
muttered, "there will always be this. Look at it.
Think what it is."

My first fear had been that the water was shipless;
it was not. Away on the Yonkers side, towards Tarrytown, was a schooner of some size tied up at a wharf;
I had heard, too, that the River-steamer-service to
Albany and back had not yet stopped for the winter.

In time I was to know much of that River pretty
well. Nothing in it is more splendid than the reach
I saw then.

"Earth has not anything to shew more fair."

Beautiful as that day was, it was nothing to Sundays
which followed, when the miles of woodland took on
the colours of the fall. I explored for many miles
up the River on the Yonkers side; the fair weather
held for many weeks, and each walk was a revelation.
I had never before been at liberty in Nature; I had
never before seen Nature at liberty and in such pro-
fusion. It was like walking into Paradise just when
I was gladdest of the happiness.

I could walk almost at once into primitive wood-land on leaving my lodgings. I had but to walk fifty yards, then I was in the woods. I had but to go a hundred yards more, up a little hill, then I was deep in the woods, out of sight of any house, shut in by scarlet sumach bushes, hundreds of them, redder than blood, and apparently belonging to nobody. Then, presently, the sumachs gave place to maples, such as I had not thought possible.

I had not seen the Indian Summer; if I had seen maples, I had seen only one or two. Here, there were hundreds together of the colours of beds of tu-lips, of green, brown, scarlet and purple in every pos-sible variety. Deep in the wood, seemingly far from anywhere, I came upon one clump which amazed me. During the fall I went to it every Sunday, for I had never seen such radiant colour upon any trees nor in any flowers. At first I thought that the beauty was not going to cease, but to change continually to something better. At last, the leaves turned to in-tense gold; then, quite suddenly, they were not there. In the next fall I visited them again. Perhaps I was older or duller; perhaps the magic in the trees was not so perfect, or the season worse; I never saw them so perfect as in the first year.

In coming home from these days in the woods, I used to try to reach the ridge of the hill at sunset, so that I could stand in a clearing or on a rock and watch the sun going down over the Palisades. The beauty

of those cliffs above the River took a hold upon me
not easy to describe. I did not know it, but somewhere over there, not far from me, were people who
were afterwards to be great friends; I have often
thought of that since then. At the time, I used to say
to myself, that the sun was going down on his way
to England, and that before I saw him again he would
have roused the cocks in the English roosts, and risen
over England and then come flooding across the grey
sea to where I was. Many a time, I watched the sun
going down behind those cliffs; and bade him take
my love here. I had heard many and many a crowd
heaving round to the rapturous cry:

> "And we love the Sun the better, since he shines
>   on England's shore."

When a mind is very empty it is astonishing how important its few contents may become.

When I returned from one of these excursions I
felt that indeed my lot had fallen on a fair ground and
that I had a goodly heritage; beauty all round me,
leisure, such as I had not thought possible, books, so
cheap that I could have a library of them, and a great,
vivid, romantic capital City only half an hour away.
In less than an hour from where I sat at my book I
could be on South Street, walking under jibbooms,
studying rigging, talking with sailors; or, if I preferred, at the Battery, looking at ships bound to England.

A poem was beginning to spread across America at that time; I can only quote from memory, I never saw it in print, and know not the right text.   I hope that I quote it correctly.

> "Sitting still and wishing
> Makes no person great,
> Good Lord sends the fishing,
> You must dig the bait."

I felt that the Lord had indeed sent marvellous fishing; but at the moment I did not know what bait to dig for, nor where to dig.   I was somewhat lost there.

During that summer, when I had been living in Greenwich Village, near the Jefferson Market Court, I had sometimes entered a book-store on Sixth Avenue, a few blocks up-town.   This store was kept by an Englishman.   In one of my visits, I had seen on his shelves a row of cheap, neat and attractive-looking books, bound in a dark slate binding with printed labels at the back.   These were the Camelot Classics, published by Walter Scott.   They cost eighteenpence the volume in England; in America, even though they were imported, they were still cheap.   I had noticed among them a volume containing the beginning of the Morte d'Arthur of Malory.   I had read about this book as being the original of some of Tennyson's Poems.   I had tried to read some of the poems, years before this, but the time was unpropitious, I had never read one right through.   Now I felt stirred to buy the

Malory. For some of the summer it was my only book. I took a good deal of pleasure in it. Though I did not know it, I was born into a decade certain to be much moved by Malory and the sentimental view of the Middle Ages. I read it, without any criticism, as a tale or succession of tales which wandered pleasantly along. I was much moved by Malory's preface, and supposed that he was right, that Arthur had lived, and that relics of him might be seen in England, at Winchester, Dover and elsewhere. It would be fun to see these, I thought. The book seemed to me to be genuine, and Tennyson's Poems seemed lifeless when set beside it.

The Malory book went with me to Yonkers: I continued to read in it, especially the tales of Merlin and of Balin and Balan.

Soon after I went to Yonkers I began to look about for book-stores, and found two, both not far from the Post Office. I went to one of these two stores every week on pay day to buy reading matter. I was not reading with system; I was much too ignorant; but I was reading steadily, and by preference work which was being done by the men of my own time.

I always bought some of the best monthly magazines, and so came to know the kind of thing demanded by them. When I considered this my heart sank; for I knew that I could never do such things.

I read the essays and despaired of ever being able to order my thoughts so neatly; the poems, feeling that

they came from a world to which I could never be admitted; and the short stories, with anguish at their
perfection.   The stories interested me most, for from
childhood I had told stories to myself or to my ship-
mates; but to write stories like these, without any unnecessary words, which got off the mark like sprinters
at the pistol, and went through with a rush to vic-
tory, seemed an art past praying for.   Some men were
born so, I judged, and the rest must just grin and bear
it.   In the magazines and newspapers I often read
comments on the contributions, and learned of magazines which might repay the reading.

Already the Americans were shewing a national genius for the short story; some of the best of their
short story writers were contributing to small monthly
and quarterly magazines made up wholly of short
stories.   I bought these, and read them carefully, with
much enjoyment and black despair mixed.   I felt that
I was ignorant of everything which might make a man
a writer.   Sometimes I took the fable of a story which
had pleased me and tried to tell it in my own way.   I
found that I had no way, and that I could not do it.

At that time, and for some years to come, America
offered a large library of the best modern fiction at
five cents or twopence halfpenny the volume.   The
books were well-printed on good paper, bound in yellow paper covers.   All the best English authors could
be had in these volumes.   I bought about twenty of
them every week, and from them soon came to know

the best work of living English novelists. The sales
of these books were probably enormous, for one saw
them everywhere; but I have often wondered since
then how they could be made and sold at a profit. I
suppose that they were sold to the retailers at something
under four cents a copy, and out of something less
than four cents the publisher had to buy the paper,
pay his printers, give, as I hope, a large percentage to
his author, and keep his office staff and himself. That
he made a profit I do not doubt, for the list of the
library was long and the firm continued in business.
I once asked an American printer how it was done.
He said, "You have to figure those things pretty close."

These cheap novels were to have considerable influence on my life.

When I had been at Yonkers for a few weeks I found
in one of my magazines an illustrated article on the
Arthurian legend; this contained some account of
Glastonbury, a photograph of the Tor, and told the
legends current at Cadbury and the Camel villages,
supposed by some to be "Camelot." This article delighted me, both for what it told and what it suggested.
Arthur lived long ago, and very little was or could be
known about him; it ought to be possible for even an
ignorant man to know that little. Thinking thus, I
wondered, if it might not be possible to get to know
all the literature of the sea. I had been carefully
trained in the obsolete seamanship; I had had practical experience of the seamanship of my own time, and

therefore had the grounding.   On the *Conway*, I had read most of the books of Marryat, Captain Chamier, R. H. Dana, and Clark Russell.   As I supposed, there were but two others, Cupples and Herman Melville.

With the hope that I might speedily master the Arthur subject, I wrote to a big firm of New York booksellers asking if they could tell me what books were published on it.   The firm replied with a charming letter and a bibliography of 200 titles which they had then in stock, adding that if their stock did not hold what I wanted, they would be delighted to search further for me.   I was somewhat dashed by the complexity of what I had thought might be a simple study. I ordered a complete Malory, and a copy of a translation of the Mabinogion.   I read the Malory straight through, with growing pleasure.   The last book enchanted me; it is certainly one of the best efforts of English story-telling.   After the muddle, mess, repetition and fantasy of most of the work, this last book has order, growth and tragical feeling.   I liked the Mabinogion much less, but as I believed then that the tales were ancient, possibly contemporary with Arthur, I gave them due respect.   That Arthur had lived, I did not then doubt.   I had even hope that some old manuscript might turn up to prove it.

In following up my wish to know the literature of the sea, I went to my Sixth Avenue bookseller and bought *The Green Hand* and two or three of the books of Herman Melville.   *The Green Hand* was not much use to me, but I liked *White Jacket* and that masterly account of New Bedford in *Moby Dick*. One other book was bought at that time, an Indian's study of Gautama the Enlightened, with an account of Buddhism. This book I read with joy, both for the beauty of the tale and the happiness of the teaching. The story of Buddha began to be a daily part of my thought and his person more and more a reality to me.

But in the mill in those weeks the interest of men was turned upon two very different persons. A man who lived near Yonkers, a man whose house we had all seen, and whose person was familiar to some of us, was to fight Robert Fitzsimmons, the English heavyweight, and the question was put daily, will he win? It was an important question, because it was felt that the winner would be entitled to challenge J. J. Corbett, the heavy-weight champion of the world. The local feeling ran high in favour of Peter Maher whose punch was said to come like the kick of a mule. One man told me that Peter could punch a hole in a brick wall. Well, I knew that Mr. Maher must be a good man, to have reached his position; but I had my own reasons for favouring the other. The battle was brief, and though Peter Maher landed a punch which made Fitzsimmons tell a journalist, "for a moment I thought I was gone," this triumph was brief as the summer flower. From that moment the mill talked daily of what would happen if and when Fitzsimmons met Corbett.

It was at about this time that a sad change came upon my happiness; the winter set in.

I have had experience of six or seven New York winters; I find them severe; as I did in that my first winter. It is true that the bitter cold is rare, and that often there are bright days of exquisite glitter and glory. My quarrel with the winter was, that it gave few days in which one could walk for pleasure. There was too much snow, the wind was too cutting, the roads were all hard ice or some combination of these things killed the fun of going out. Then, the River was frozen, and in the woods the granite stuck out of the snow like old bones. All the colour and the joy seemed dead. In the mill they shut the great windows and turned on the steam heat, which was snug, no doubt, and even necessary for some of the processes, but exceedingly unpleasant to myself, who would rather be frozen than stuffy. I found the change to steam heat very trying and the sudden removal of natural beauty hard to bear. Another point against the winter was that we had no daylight to ourselves save on Sundays; we went in the dark and cold to the steam-heat, and walked back in the dark and cold when the day was done. Still, when I did get back, since I had no wish to walk in the dark and cold, there were consolations waiting for me. I settled in for the evening; lit my little oil-stove, and read some modern masterpiece, or made a foolish attempt to do what some skilled writer had done well in one of my maga-

zines. I know that in the first of the winter evenings
I was very lonely, since I was now deprived of the
overwhelming natural beauty which had rejoiced my
heart when I had first come there. If I had felt lonely
then I had but to walk into the woods or to sight of
the River, and all my troubles would fall away. Well,
there was no sense in being too lonely so near to a
splendid city like New York. In New York, only a
short train ride from me, were some acquaintances,
theatres, music-halls and the incomparable lighted,
thrilling exciting streets. Those were the days for
music-halls all over the world; New York had two very
good ones; she offered to me, also, another delight, a
great variety of shipping.

Though I longed to be quit of the sea, so that I
might study other things, I had and have a passion
for ships and all to do with them. I had been mixed
up with ships and sailors for years; they had made my
life, they were my only knowledge, they had given
me my only friends. I could spend all day looking
at ships, looking at one ship, or one mast of a ship.
These things were the marvellous works of art of that
time; they were its dynamic thought.

In those days, the sailing-ship was swiftly ending;
she was losing market after market; and in the struggle
had been made cheap, simple, tank-like, and as we call
it "parish-rigged." Still, in every big port, there were
survivors of a grander time, of only a few years before,
when the noble four-master brought the ship to her

last perfection, and the lofty wooden full-rigged American clipper maintained the traditions of Donald McKay.

New York, the marvellous City, had then the best display of ships in the world. Perhaps the very best of the display was on South Street. My favourite beat was West Street, which has been compared with Circular Quay at Sydney; but Circular Quay could never have held a third of the ships. There was a street on the water-front at San Francisco, just under the Barbary Coast, which ran it close, perhaps, but that too, was less capacious. Liverpool Docks usually held more ships, but they were shut from the life of the city into a world of docks. In West Street, though they were beginning to build the great covered warehouses which now hide so many berths, the ships still came right up to the Street, so that in places you could walk under jibbooms and figureheads, and trip over hawsers. You could really see the ships and take stock of them. In one reach of the street, close together, were the berths of the big Liverpool steamers; further down town were sailing ships of all sorts and steamship lines plying to the south; further down town still you came to the Battery, where pretty Jenny Slattery at that time dwelt, before being married at Casey's; at the Battery you got a blow from the sea, and could see the Harbour with its islands, its many ferries, the great ships coming in or going out, and Liberty Enlightening the World.

Many of the ships were old friends; I had seen them often before, had gone over them, and aloft in them. All the big Liverpool steamers were known to me; I knew their records and rotation.

The ships which charmed me with their novelty were the big soft-wood American five- and six-masted schooners, which I had never before seen at close-quarters. I was also deeply interested in the wooden American sailing ships, of which there were many, some of them pretty old, of great interest to me, because of various differences in rig and survivals of ancient practice. Many of these ships were in exquisite trim, having newly come home to their port of ownership with their rigging tarred down, their paintwork bright, and their yards square by the lifts and braces.

I have never been able to see a well-kept ship without longing to be adding my mite to her fair appearance. As I walked that avenue of ships I know that I was often stirred by the longing to be a rigger, employed all day in a rigging loft or in ships fitting for sea, yet having my nights free for study. That seemed to me to be a fair life, to be working about ships all day and at books for half the night. But I knew a good deal about a rigger's life; I had known lots of riggers, and I knew that there were three things against my being a rigger; I was not nearly old enough; I had not the experience; and these two faults made the third, that I was not nearly good enough as a practical seaman. I had seen some old Liverpool riggers, the salt of the profession; how could I hope to do what those men did, in wire-splicing, roping of courses, or cutting shrouds from the coil? How could I do what they did so easily with fids, heavers and those fingers, once compared with fish-hooks, but now to be compared with pliers, levers and spanners combined? It was sad, but I could not be a rigger.

I cannot quite recollect how it came to pass, but I learned that on West Street there was a little Seamen's Mission, which had a reading-room in which simple church services were sometimes held. I suppose that I came upon the place in one of my wanderings, looking at the ships. It must have been November, when I learned of it. The next week-end, I went there with a great pile of my five-cent novels, as many as I could carry. These I left for the seamen in need of something to read. I said that I would bring more later on, and did so. I used to go there with books whenever I went to New York. On this first visit, I went from the Mission to the bookshop on Sixth Avenue, where I bought two books. One of them was a five-cent copy of Walton's *Angler* of which I had read praise in some magazine. I read some of it, with delight in the verses quoted, and some faint pleasure in Venator and the milkmaid; but hot indignation against Piscator for his beastly cruelty to frogs and worms. I have never read beyond the first few pages; to me, the book is a davender, a davender or dub.

The other book was George Du Maurier's *Trilby.*

Since those days, a few books have become household names all over the world. I remember at least half a dozen which have been sold by the hundred thousand and are still selling; but no book that I can call to mind has caused the stir made by *Trilby* in that year. You were reminded of the book everywhere, in shop-windows, in shoes, boots and slippers, newspapers, magazines, sermons, talk, and the catchwords of the avenue. Collars, hats, toothpastes, cosmetics, corn-cures, foods, and I know not what other things were named from it or from characters in the book. The word "foot" was put almost out of use: a familiar kind of hat received the new name. The forgotten song of Ben Bolt was revived; everybody hummed it; every barrel-organ played it; every contralto on the halls sang it. Popular songs were made about Trilby: everybody sang them; the knock-about comedians joked about her in their patter. There were Trilby dolls, and big Trilby figures and figurines. I had long wanted to know what all this stir meant; now I learned.

I was told that one man who had collected all the press-cuttings about the book had refused twenty thousand dollars for the collection, and that he would have been a fool had he taken the offer.

On the whole, I enjoyed it more than any book I

had read until that time; but partly because the illustrations and the uncanny figure of Svengali reminded me of overwhelming instants in my childhood, when I had brooded upon old volumes of *Punch*, in which that romantic Jew had appeared often enough in other forms (and the romantic view of France as well). Youth longs for close companionships. The book described an enchanted companionship of men linked together in the practice of art; it gave me, therefore, the image of a double happiness. It gave me moreover an impression of France which I have never lost, and quoted to me, for the first time, scraps of French verse which seemed very beautiful. I told myself, that I was indeed ignorant, that I knew nothing of English and less than nothing of French; yet here was France apparently wiser and richer in beauty than most lands, and there was I, not knowing one line of what she had created.

I bought a French grammar and dictionary, and, as *Trilby* mentions the book, the *Trois Mousquetaires;* with these, and other Dumas, I began to improve my French. The book refers to Sterne's *Sentimental Journey*, and to Darwin's *Origin of Species;* I bought those, too, and some school editions of the comedies of Molière. These were very well in their way, but the poems quoted in *Trilby* seemed to come from deeper wells nearer the world's end. I felt, that I was not yet where Du Maurier had been; I was still in the desert while he was in the garden. One very beauti-

ful poem quoted in the book had a refrain which said
that the wind blowing across the mountain would
drive the speaker mad. Who had written that and
what was the rest of it?

Almost at once, while I was in this happiness, I
heard a man say that he could not understand all this
fuss about *Trilby;* it was nothing at all to *Peter Ibbetson.*

This remark must have been made in November.
I remember with what fever I waited till I could buy
Peter Ibbetson, and how I bore the volume home,
opened it at the drawing of the little child wheeling
a barrow from the Past into the Future, and at once
drew measurably nearer to the garden of romance.
I have read that book through many times since then.
God forgive me, once or twice I have wondered
whether there be not one or two faults in it; if there
be, there were none to me then. It came to me just
when I most needed an inner life. On the whole,
no prose story not even *Don Quixote,* has given me
one fifth part of the pleasure and mental companionship. From the book, I learned, that there was a
French poet named de Musset, whom I ought to
know, and one François Villon who had written a
Ballade of Dead Ladies. I bought a de Musset and
a Villon, but the time was not ripe for either.

As in the reading of *Trilby,* I was often entranced
in *Peter Ibbetson* by little drawings, which suggested
the scenes of earlier enchantments in the pages of

Punch. I am afraid that it did not come into my mind to write to thank the author of this delight; if it did, I put the thought aside, feeling that it would be cheek, or that he would have praise enough from his friends, or that he would be weary of letters from strangers; indeed, I had read that he had been overcome by the success of *Trilby.* I did not write to thank him, and have grieved for it many times. When I came to London, I used often to go to Hampstead, so that I might pass by his grave and thank him as I passed. I could never pass his old home there without the deepest feelings of gratitude.

With *Peter Ibbetson,* the steam-heat of the mill and the darkness of the winter days were marvellously cheered, and other solaces were coming. In my reading I had often come upon a phrase, which I have not lately met with. A certain kind of writer would in those days use some such words as "had I the pen of a De Quincey," or "had I the opium-tinted imagination of De Quincey." I began to wonder, who was this De Quincey, and what sort of a pen had he? If he were such a splendid pen, then, perhaps, I might learn from him something of the art of being a pen. I needed all the guidance that could be had, perhaps he could supply some. It was easy to buy *The Confessions of an Opium Eater* for a few cents. I read the book with much feeling; the pages describing London streets at night seemed to me to be profound. It was from this book that I made my first acquaintance with

Shelley and Wordsworth, whom De Quincey quotes.
I learned the quotations by heart and often said them
over to myself, as I worked at the setts, but had no
thought of buying their works. Instead, I bought
another De Quincey book, *Murder as a Fine Art,* an
admirable work, which will give any sensitive reader
a lively sense of his throat on any dark night on any
road. Then another delight came to me; at a time
when I was having a lot of delights, but as yet not
really knowing what delight in its fullness meant. I
had for some months been a regular subscriber to a
merry illustrated New York paper called *Truth,* in no
way like the English paper of that name, except that
it published a Christmas Number which everybody
read.

In the usual way, I bought the Christmas Number
of this American *Truth,* and read it through. It had
in it, with some illustrations of phantasy, a longish
narrative poem by Duncan Campbell Scott, called *The
Piper of Arll.* This was the first poem by a living
writer to touch me to the quick. It was narrative;
it was delicate phantasy; it was about the sea and singing and a romantic end. I did not know it at the
time, but it was a choice example of the work of the
romantic poets of that decade. Its longing, its wist-
fulness and the perfection of some of its images made
deep impressions on me. I read it till I knew it by
heart; even now, I often repeat it to myself. Years
later I came upon the writing of a critic who men-

tions it as a poem "the symbolism of which escapes
me." Well, let it escape. The romantic mood and
the dream may be of deep personal significance and
joy, even if the author's thought elude us. I used to
repeat the poem mentally as I stood at the sides of
setts, looking along the lines of tiny tin tubes. I could
see Arll, the cove, the pines upon the hill; and the
strange ship coming in and presently sinking down.
In that mood, she could have done no other than sink,
and all my years with sailors failed to make me call
for a Court of Enquiry into her sinking.

I have said little about life in the mill during these
days because it was unvarying; one day told another.
I went in the dark to my breakfast in the Restaurant,
walked in the dark to the mill, arrived a minute or
two before seven and passed the day pulling out setts,
going carefully over them, marking them O.K. (for
Orl Krect) and taking them to the elevator where
Perce would ask if I thought The Battling Cowboy
could whip Jim Pug, or if Jim would ever grow to be
a champ. I lunched in the mill, leaning against a
wool-rack, and afterwards read a newspaper. At six
in the evening I walked in the dark to my Restaurant
and so home to my books. The work was unceasing
throughout the day, but when the whistle blew, it was
done; I was free.

I thought the work easy, even trivial; but I had
begun to see what it amounted to. Let it be understood that I was glad of it, since it gave me so much

for which I had longed for years, but I was now considering it as that friend had advised me, as a possible way of life. I had already had some little success in the mill; I had heard that I was praised; and I had had a raise, as we called it; I was earning more money.

Business, as far as we could see, was improving. The games of curling in the lunch-hour had come to an end, for the office had been shifted from our floor to a space in the middle of the setting-room above us. Our own floor was being swiftly altered, so as to make of it two floors instead of one. They put over our heads a floor in which they built racks for the storage of completed set spools waiting to be woven. They also moved the cutters and the men of my section across to the western side of the building, so that we looked out on the big bare hill, instead of on the smoke of the dyeing rooms.

I now began to see what chance I had of further promotion. I had begun with the ambition of learning all the processes in use, so that I could bear a hand in all or any of them. That I found was impossible. When we were busy, as we were, my job kept me engaged all day long; I saw next to nothing of any other process, except the cutting. I learned the dodge of cutting; it took one minute to learn, after that the only problem connected with it, was to cut fast enough to make a good week's pay, while not cutting so fast as to cause the rate to be reduced. I had watched Perce with the elevator, and though I had never

worked it for myself, I judged that I could do it, if
asked. The only other jobs in my section were taking out setts from the racks, which needed more
strength than skill, and mending the spool-ends with
glue; I judged that I could do both those jobs. But
the main work of my part of the mill was the weaving.
When we were busy, we hardly ever went to the
weaving-floors, save when we took some special sett to
a waiting loom, and then only to leave the sett and
return. I had never been to the setting-room nor to
the picking-room; I knew nothing of either floor. The
looms were the centre of our industry, and I began to
fear that I should never have a chance of learning how
they worked, and how they differed. I had taken to
reaching the mill a few minutes before seven in the
morning. By taking different routes to my section I
had contrived to see all the weaving sections, and had
noted the main types of loom in use, and the different
types of carpet woven on them. When the power was
fully on these looms were thundering with a roaring
racket like a battle; the air and the floor were thick
with wool-dust; and lads with wide-headed brooms
were everywhere, trying to keep the gangways free
from it. When I went through them before the power
was fully on, the noise was only a bickering hum, with
a jerking jangle and bang from the chains and swords.
It was not possible to stop to examine anything, only
guard' e pass', yet I noted and marvelled; and again
had the feeling that the great vertical strips of woven

carpet behind every loom shewed how the stuff should be used, as wall-decoration, not as covering for floors, to be trodden underfoot and hardly noticed. I saw enough to convince me that a loom was a most intricate machine, needing a world of toil before it would weave, yet fascinating in every detail. I longed especially to see what happened when my own work ended; in this, I was disappointed; in all the time I was there, I never once saw the setts being put into the chains.

I was disappointed that I could not learn more of the work in its earlier and later stages. At odd times, during the mid-day break, I questioned one of the cutters who had been in the mill for many years, in several sections. He reckoned up more than thirty processes through which each carpet had to pass; even so, some were unknown to him. He put the total number at about thirty-seven, but judged it might be more rather than less. It was by this time plain to me that unless I were moved to a section, I could not learn its process. The visiting of other sections was impossible in working hours and almost impossible out of them; strangers were not welcome anywhere. I was told that the setting-rooms above my floor were interesting; once or twice, I was there for a moment in the day-time; it was a place of great business, with a good deal of rattle and chatter; very light, and much shut off into compartments. I was told that the picking-room in the basement was the place where I should see the fin-

ished carpet before it left the mill; however, it was
not possible for me to go to the picking-room; it was
but a name to me; it had a good name, as being the
best of all the floors; with good light, no dust and no
noise.

As I could not learn other processes than those close
to me, and as I now did my own work mechanically,
with an attention and care which could be detached
as slaves to the task while my mind amused itself
with other matters, I began to devise mental delights
to keep me going through the day. I remembered
the page in *Two Years before the Mast* in which
R. H. Dana describes how he wiled away the long
night-watches. My own watches were longer than his,
and had not the blessed marking of the bells at every
half hour. As my only exact knowledge at that time
was of ships and the sea, my first device was to set myself problems in seamanship, start a course of action, in-
terpose various checks and difficulties, meet these, one
by one, and finally beat down Satan under my feet.
These for a time worked very well; they would last
me for hours. I remember propounding to myself
the following problems:—"You have been dismasted
in a flush-decked vessel; your new spars have been
floated alongside; how will you proceed to get them
on board?"
or "You are running-free, making eight or nine knots,
when a man falls overboard from the foreyard. What
steps will you take and why?"

or "Falconer advises against the embrailing of the lee-yard-arm. Are you of his opinion? Give reasons for and against this practice."
or "Describe the formation and life-history of an area of low pressure in the northern hemisphere."
or "You are homeward bound in the North Atlantic in January, the wind S.E., the barometer falling rapidly; how will you proceed?"
or "You are sent aloft to send down the sky sail and royal yards, with the mast after the yards. Describe what you will do in detail, in the proper order."

Other recreations were the Rule of the Road at Sea, which I could repeat by heart, the rhymes by Gray on that theme, and the Channel Lights, going either to Liverpool or to London from the westward. I often "boxed the compass," first right-handed, then left-handed, then in zig-zags, four points here and there.

One amusement, which lasted a long time, was the going over the rigging of a mast or masts, from the truck to the partners. Rigging is a fascinating subject. As it chanced, I had a fair knowledge of the latest and best practices of the Navy and the Merchant Service, with this exception, that I had not seen studdingsail gear rove or used. Apart from studdingsail gear, which was obsolete when I was young (though I often saw ships with the boom-irons at the yard-arms) I could start at the truck and go gradually down the mast, pausing at each yard to go out to the yard-arm and name each thing on my way, then laying-in and going on down, describing each part of standing rigging and the lead of all the running rigging. On the whole, I preferred the modern Merchant Service practice, so powerful, simple and grand, so full of hope (or so it seemed to sailors) that that dangerous element the sea was being slowly overcome. Yet when I went over a Naval mast of, say, 1865, reflecting that those enormous spars were made of wood, and supported by hemp, and that those gigantic sails had been reefed and furled by men in a few minutes, I knew that that system had been one of great splendour. I knew what years of thought had gone to create it, and what skill of hand went to the fitting of each thing, what perfection of craft and beauty of work.

When these delights had come to an end, I could always go over books or chapters which had pleased me. Often, after the mid-day break, I had something from the newspaper to reflect upon; then there were always the problems put by Perce or another, whether such an one, heavy-weight or middle-weight, would beat somebody else. From the talk of my fellows, I came to know something of all the eminent boxers of the time.

With these mental amusements, and a great press of work, the days slipped by to Christmas, without much change. I know that before Christmas, I often thought of those lines on the engraving of Ulysses and the Sirens, and wondered how to get the rest of the poem. Somehow, I discovered that they came from Pope's Odyssey which could easily be bought for a few cents, so I bought it, in a neat edition with the designs of John Flaxman. It is said, that the Twelfth Book containing the Siren passage, is the work of William Broome.

In those days, the work of the eighteenth century was disliked, save perhaps by a few professors. I found the couplet and the jargon unpleasing; and was by no means skilled enough to perceive the perfection of much of the verse. But I found the story worth the trouble, and enjoyed getting to know in full the incidents which had been so often mentioned in reviews, newspaper articles and literary comment. As I went on, I was more deeply moved; the passage of the Sirens delighted me, and the last third of the poem struggled through its distasteful dress and made me think that it must be a fine thing.

At this time, I read somewhere, that the Spectator Essays of Steele and Addison were models of English prose. I bought these, too, and read them carefully. When I tried to put their matter into my own words, I could have wept at my incompetence.

That season was made anxious by international tensions. President Cleveland had commented on our dealings with Venezuela, and his comment had been followed by other comment in the press. This comment supported the President in his contention, that the Monroe Doctrine should be upheld. Perhaps, ex-

perienced statesmen thought little of the breeze; some
of the newspapers made a good deal of it, and talked
of war, and what would be done if war came.   My
lot, as an enemy alien, might not have been bright; I
was therefore a good deal worried.   However, the
breeze died down, and all was quiet on the Potomac,
when the news came that Dr. Jameson had led a raid
against the Boers.

Our forward policy, as it was called, in South Africa,
and our noisy blowing of the Imperial trumpet for
some years without intermission, had won us many
enemies all over the world.   To the American people, the raid seemed like a lawless attempt against a
simple God-fearing race of farmers; I suppose that it
was universally condemned; such comment as I saw
was outspoken, and very bitter, against us.   The raiders were soon rounded-up and put into pen.   The
feeling roused against us in Europe was intense.   Sitting in the mill, three thousand miles away, I read
the European comment, unanimously hostile, and
marvelled that we should be so misunderstood.   There
followed some anxious, bitter weeks, during which my
country and her foreign policies were lampooned and
caricatured throughout the world.   Since then, one
of the raiders had told me that the raid might have
had more success, if two troopers detailed to cut tele-
graph wires had cut them, instead of cutting a wire-
fence by mistake.   Another said that when in the
prison camp, he had but one pair of socks, which he

washed one at a time, lest thieves should be tempted by the pair.

The days after Christmas were cold, dark and hateful; no doubt many of the days were bright, but so little daylight was free. A stranger in a land not his own has often a kind of inverted home-sickness or touchiness about his nation; I certainly had. The international comment upon England would not have bothered me had I been in England; where I was, I had daily to hear criticisms and alien points of view, which made me suffer acutely. It did me good to discover that this land is but one of many, and that her wisdom or way is not the only one in the world. Still, while I was learning, I did not think that it did me good, for the discovery was not made at once, it came to me slowly, with a lot of pain.

I went sometimes to New York. Usually, when I went, I brought a package of novels to the Seamens' Mission, and sometimes talked or played draughts with the seamen. One of them shewed me a frightful wound in his leg, which he said was growing worse, and what ought he to do with it? Another told me how he had been adrift on a grating, or hatch-cover, for three days near Cuba. Another offered to sell me a watch, which I'm sorry to say had no works. I had seen a number of such watches during the summer and did not trade.

I remember being in New York on one day of frightful cold, when the roads and side-walks were caked

with hard ice, and an appalling blast was blowing
straight from the North Pole. It was a Sunday, yet
there, close to me, was an English full-rigged ship of
about 1400 tons, with hands aloft on all three masts,
sending down the royal and topgallant masts and
yards. Either something had been sprung, or, more
probably, she was making ready to go under Brook-
lyn Bridge. What the cold of the wind must have
been on the cross-trees, I shudder to think; it was
probably nearly zero where I was. I could not keep
from watching her and them, for the thing seemed of
unusual importance, and lay within my scanty personal knowledge.

During two years of training, I had often and often
been aloft, sending down the *Conway's* topgallant
yards and masts. It was a job which we had reduced
to a fine art, for the gear was light, simple and exactly
suited to our routine. Half a dozen neat swift acts
sufficed to send the yard on deck; a few more brought
the mast down; then we would reverse the process
and up they would go; the fore working against the
main, and everybody enjoying every minute of it.
We had been told by our officers and instructors that
in THEIR day, this business was routine at dusk in
all ships.

It had long since ceased to be routine in any ship.
Those poor fellows aloft in the freezing blast were
working with spanners on nuts, where we had worked
with fingers on toggles; they were dealing with great

weights and an infinite complexity of gear, and were doing it in some cases, no doubt, for the first time for years. I watched them with anguish and admiration, thinking "that is real glory; man is doing nothing finer than that anywhere; it passes un-noticed and the men who are aloft will neither be praised nor thanked; yet what a feat it is." I went home, wondering why the deeds of work are not heeded, while the deeds of sport fill the headlines. I had been seeing a terrible photograph of a graveyard in Darien; it was called "Little Ireland" because it contained the graves of Irish labourers, who had gone to dig the abortive French Panama Canal and had died. Why should those frost-bitten men in the cross-trees, and the dead near Culebra be disregarded while some one who gave a dance at which the dancers dressed like wild animals, or the man who wore skirts or the woman who wore trousers received columns in the press? I knew that there was some defect in the sense of value. It was borne in upon me that the seeker for truth goes into the desert, or wherever there is nothing, to correct his sense of values. Presently men would look again at bare manhood, whether in the frost or in the jungle, and would clear a lot of folly and idolatry away. I judged that in any clearing they would destroy much that was precious; for Life seemed to me to be haphazard and extraordinarily wasteful; and the Nations seemed to take no forethought for anything save evil to their neighbours.

As in most winters there, we had something which we called a blizzard. Coming back from the mill in the snow and howling norther, in a temperature of perhaps ten below zero, we could but run for it, now with our fingers over our ears, wondering if our ears were still there, then with our fingers in our mouths, wondering if the fingers were still there. The excess of any weather is exhilarating. Talking of the cold afterwards, our elders told us of the Great Blizzard of some half dozen years before, when death and destruction had swept all the Northern States; that had been a real blizzard, this was nothing but a snowstorm. I have been in some real blizzards since then, and know that they spoke truth.

After some months, when I had exercised my mind on every topic of practical seamanship within my knowledge, and had propounded questions to which I did not know the answer, I hit upon another means of wiling away the long day at the setts. I began to go over the daily routine of the *Conway*, taking whatever I felt to be good in it, and imagining what should replace those parts of the routine which were faulty. From this point I proceeded brightly to the slow creation of a great Merchant Service college, of which the *Conway* was but a part. This was the work of many days; I built it up slowly in my mind during the latter part of the winter and when I had completed the routine, I began to imagine the College, its playing fields, its docks, its slips, piers, boats, ships and engine-shops.   By March I had the buildings clearly imagined, with the flags flying and the work going forward in all its branches.   I had done the thing in style, while I was at it.   I had taken-in, cleared, excavated and completely changed some five hundred yards of the Mersey front, for the marine side of the venture, and had cleared, levelled and rebuilt the greater part of Rock Ferry for the shore buildings.   Outside Thelema there had been few such Colleges.   It was a College well worthy of a maritime people; I gave to it a great deal of excited and happy thought and though I shall not live to see its foundation-stones laid, others perhaps may.   It kept me going through a dark time.

March that year was a maddening month.   People had said, "Oh, the winter's always over by March." It is sometimes so in England.   In New York State it is wiser to reckon March as winter.   We had frequent falls of late snow that March, and though the snow did not stay it had a power of giving the lie to the growing daylight.   It was always saying: "I'm here still, the Winter; no Spring for you yet."   However, spring comes in the end, even in England; it came again to New York State; the ice disappeared from the river; the steamers began to ply; all the lovely forest budded and blossomed. Half of my troubles fell away at once, for the exhilaration of the sun returned; I could walk in the woods in daylight after work and exult in the spring.   I have always felt that Americans have more joy from their brief and beautiful spring than any people; no springs have given me more joy than theirs. In the happy influence of sun and blossoms, the steam-heat went from the mill; the windows were opened, and my Service College became daily more splendid in some detail or other. I built and rigged a barquentine and a small, very perfect, full-rigged ship, for the use of the senior students. When these had been taken over I began to fill the imaginary buildings with staff and boys, some five hundred or so. All that imagining was delightful to me, and perhaps useful; it helped me to make precise images, to reject unfitting images, and to make the thing complete in each detail, each door and window fitted in the proper place, nothing left vague, and nothing admitted that was not choicely good.

As I had no knowledge of building costs, save as they affected ships and their masts, sails and engines, I could not say what my College would cost to build, endow and work. I have sometimes been blamed for not thinking more of this side of a question. However, I have come to know that money is largely a fiction, and that if there be the Will to have a splendid thing, that thing will be made. A Nation is great just in so far as she wills to have splendid things; if she wills them, they come; if she does not, she will mess along with anything which will somehow do. Anyhow, we were said to be the richest Nation in the world, and were beyond all question the people most occupied with sea-affairs. If we did not presently wake up and build such a College, now that the rule-of-thumb days were done, we were like to get a jolt from life.

While I was working at the details of this College, I had the news of the trouble of a friend. He was some thousands of miles away, and the news turned my thought to him, away from my fantasies. It seemed to me likely that he might need any money I could spare, and that I had better begin to save at once. I began to save; I changed my way of life to something more thrifty, and in my spare time wrote to this friend devising comforts. In the mill, my thoughts were usually turned to him. I began soon to know what intense power thought has, when it is mixed with friendship. At one time, I felt that perhaps it would be better to go to him, although the journey was not an easy one to make. I went to New York and asked at the Seamen's Mission, if they could ship me a part of the way and find out for me how I could proceed from that point. They knew all the firms likely to be of help for the first part of the journey; they very kindly enquired for me and discovered that business was slack; that it was useless to expect a berth; and that even if I reached the central point my chance of getting further by sea was remote. This dashed my hopes of going to him and added to my anxiety about him. I continued to save money in case he should want it; and presently his affairs took a much brighter

turn, so that his trouble ended, while mine took a turn
for the worse.

I had been hoping for some promotion in the mill,
short as my time had been there. I believe that I had
had my money increased twice, if not three times, but
this was not enough for the greed and the vanity of
youth; I hoped for a markedly better job, and had begun to think that one was preparing for me. It would
have been a pleasant job, too. I knew that someone
was going to be promoted, that his old job would be
given at once to someone, and one or two men let me
know (on insufficient grounds) that I was thought of
for the post. This was a great delight to me; and I
was still young enough to count chickens before they
hatched. I had never taken to heart a seaman's proverb. "Don't hope; then you won't be disappointed."
I did hope; and I was bitterly disappointed, when the
job was given to one older and in every way more competent than myself, who had been in the mill an even
shorter time than myself. It was a cruel blow to me.
Youth gets a good many such on its way to sense. I
was in despair.

"Enough of all this" I thought. "This is a sign
that I shall never get along here; I shall be passed over
and disappointed again. I had better get out of this
and go again to sea, and give up thought of learning
the carpet-business, and trying to write."

I went again to New York, to ask, if I could be

shipped, I did not much care where. However, my luck was in, the business depression was on the port, so they told me; shipping was slack and seamen plenty, besides, who wanted a boy? I remembered one runner who said "Shipping's on de hog fer fair." There was nothing doing, which was something of a comedown for one who had built so fine a Merchant Service college. I went back, feeling that since I could not get away I had better stay where I was; but the interest was gone from the work; I was very unhappy, and my unhappiness was soon made worse. The man who won the promotion only held it for about a fortnight. He asked for an afternoon off, went to New York, came back drunk, and roused the burg with outrageous disorder. He was sacked next morning; but his bishopric did another take; I was passed over again. I told myself, I didn't care; but I did care, intensely. They might have tried me at the job, for the new man was sacked within a few days, which I should not have been.

But even this second ruin of their hopes did not teach them sense; plainly the gods had made them witless; they passed me by once more and put in another; however, it was no good troubling further about such people; if they did not know their own advantage, they must suffer accordingly. I gave up hoping for that particular job; it wasn't anything of a job anyway. I do not even remember who had it, nor if he kept it.

I was now almost at the gates of a great experience, and was in the misery in which travellers approach such places. Since all the ways seemed impossible, the chances were that it was I who was impossible; others had trodden them all, yet I could tread none. I had almost given up trying to write; the results were so sad; and one trouble or another had poisoned my summer.

It fell, that I met two men, who had worked their way through an American College, and had taken degrees. They told me that many American Colleges made it possible for men to work their way, attend classes and take degrees. They said that such men worked in vacations and at stated times on the College Farms, did odd jobs about the College, even ran some of the College Departments at a fair wage, and could in these ways take all the classes, and qualify for any profession. This seemed to me like a tale of fairyland; but I found that it was true. Quite close to me, in New York and just across the River in New Jersey, there were Colleges which took people on these terms. I remember well the ecstasy with which I thought of this as I worked at the setts. I could perhaps study Medicine, qualify as a doctor and lead a life useful to others. The two men said that it would be possible, but that it would take me six or seven years, since Medicine was a long course, and if you earned your living at the same time, it took much longer than usual. It would be hard work, they said. Well, I was used to hard work, leading nowhere; I was not going to shrink from it when it led to knowledge, and mental peace. But the question rose up in my mind. "I am English. These advantages are for Americans. I shall probably not be eligible, or, if I be, then I shall be bound in honour to become an American citizen. Still if they give me these amazing advantages, I ought not to mind that; I ought to give that loyalty in return."

I wrote to two Colleges not far from me. From both I received the assurance that nationality was no bar; they were there to offer knowledge to students. Liberty was in fact enlightening the world. But now the blow fell upon me, that I was of an ignorance shameful for my age. I was years behind ninety-nine out of every hundred beginning medical students. It was true that I knew a good deal of obsolete seamanship, and some modern practice; I could navigate, and could pass a stiff examination in *Trilby, Peter Ibbetson* and *The Piper of Arll;* but I knew no chemistry whatever, and had no glimmering of any science not connected with the sea. With despair and hope conflicting in my mind, I bought a Gray and some elementary chemistry-books. I began painfully to win some crumbs of Anatomy, Physiology and other knowledge, not enough to make much difference to my ignorance, but enough to shew me how lovely a Queen knowledge is. I said to myself, "I believe I can do this; it will be a long pull; but it can be done." One of my two informants told me that a man at their College had made lots of money while at College by writing advertisements. Alas, every head that I heard of seemed to be of a different shape from mine and to be much better filled.

On Sundays, I took my walks up the River, or into the woods. Sometimes I talked a little over a fence with a farm-hand, but usually, as it was Sunday, the farm men would be sleeping; and I would meet no one.

The River and the woods were an unending joy to me; and the great sun of the American summer seemed to swelter down joy day after day.

Sometimes, in the moonlit summer evenings, it was too hot to sit indoors under a lamp; it was pleasanter to wander out along one of the avenues. On some of these, there were places where one could sit or lean, under the trees, to watch the great moths beating at the arc-lamps, or the fireflies in their beauty. I could never tire of the miracle of the fireflies.

While sitting thus one evening, I was joined by a West Indian who was slightly known to me. We fell into talk together. Presently, we were joined by a stranger, whom I remember clearly, though I never saw him again. He was a dapper, well-preserved man of about fifty-five, with a pale face and singularly bright eyes. Like us, he was trying to find a little coolness.

The West Indian began to talk about his childhood in the islands. "There is always wind," he said, "from the land and sea-breezes; and everybody in the islands flies kites. We always fixed bits of broken glass to our strings, and when we saw a dandier kite than ours, we would try to sidle our string with the glass upon it up against its string, so as to cut it and bring it down." This brought him to remember some of the consequences of this kind of thing, and from this he began to tell us what friends of his, then living in Yonkers, had at some time or other killed people. He mentioned six without pausing; then, after some thought, he named three more. "Then there's Mr. ⸻; he's killed his man." The bright-eyed man said, slowly, "I don't know whether I've killed anybody or not. I hope not; but I've tried often enough. I was two years in the artillery during the War." He did not seem inclined to tell us about the War; but went on "After it was over, I didn't seem able to settle down. I was knocking around a long time, and at last went to Africa. I got into another war there, as a wagon-driver, against the Zulus. Now the Zulus were the finest body of men I've ever seen. They were all big, fine men, and most of them had plumes on their heads, or held their long shields up, to look like plumes. When they did that, and charged, you thought each man was at least eight feet high. And yell . . . Don't you ever mock at a war-cry . . . I heard the Rebel Yell, and those fellows. They say Red Indians yell, too; it always seemed more of a screech to me." Here, another man took a seat among us, with the remark that we seemed to be finding a little coolness, so he would chip in and join us. His coming broke the current of talk and changed the topic. I have wondered, ever since, why that bright-eyed man thought the Red Indian cry "more of a screech." Where had he heard it? Not in Buffalo Bill's Show, I thought.

There were many veterans of the Civil War in Yonkers then. Like most soldiers, they had gone to the War amid scenes of great enthusiasm, and had come back to a long depression, and perhaps a good deal of public neglect. After thirty years, the tide turned; the survivors, with whom I talked, had begun to find themselves romantic to the young. The publication of the Century Books of Memories, and the vivid tales of Mr. Stephen Crane, had turned thousands to the study of the War, and the old soldiers found themselves beset with listeners. "Grand-père, parlez-nous de Lui." I talked with many veterans, first and last, and got from them the main impression, that if there had been no mud the war might not have been so bad. Some of them had forgotten many things, but all remembered the mud, "the mud of Virginia."

One man told me that he lay wounded for two days in a little shallow pan or hollow. An enemy cavalry patrol man saw him, and rode up to kill him. The horse was fresh and the horseman not very skilled. He rode round and round the pan, leaning from his

81

saddle and hacking at the wounded man with his sword, nicking him here and there, but never doing him much harm, and at last nicking his horse, which bolted.

All with whom I talked said that nothing in their time had been so terrible or so deeply moving as the coming of the news of the death of President Lincoln.

As it came about, I was not long left discouraged in the mill; there were a few rearrangements, from which I greatly profited. For some reason which I do not understand two new men were wanted at the job known as "taking-out setts." This work needed no particular skill, and could be quickly learned. I should think that even a stupid man could have learned it in five minutes. It was well-paid (I think on a piece-work basis), and as long as the worker were strong and attentive he could keep at it all day without mishap. It was hard work; he had to be strong to do it. There was a great deal of stooping, lifting and carrying. On a hot summer day, the constant bending and lifting between the racks and the trucks must have been very trying. Men liked the job because it was well-paid; the work was somewhat beyond the strength of a boy. Looking back at it, I can only suppose that the mill was unusually busy. A new man, an uncouth creature of enormous physical vitality, with superb arms and shoulders, was taken on and sent to take out setts. The "mistake-finder," whom I had daily seen in my section, was warned that he would be promoted to it too; promoted, because it meant a considerable increase in pay. I had not known the mistake-finder; I had only seen him flitting about. Now, quite suddenly, I was told to go to him and learn his job. If I remember rightly, I had to learn it in that day and the next, since on the day after that my teacher would be taking-out setts.

I gave up my tin-opener to a young Scot, who took my place, and set about the learning of the new mystery. It was perplexing and intricate. At once, I found that the work would take me all over the mill. Within half an hour, I had been over the setting-rooms, onto all the weaving floors, and down into the picking-room. The picking-room brought unexpected trials of a peculiar kind.

The picking-room filled about two thirds of the basement of that great building. The remaining third part of the floor was given over to some revolving mechanism of spools and spindles, winding what seemed to be loom-yarn, with a clean and dustless machinery making little noise save a low dry rattle. The remaining two thirds of the enormous floor was the picking-room proper. At the extreme northern end of it was a space for packers and shippers.

It was called the picking-room, because in it the carpets were examined when they were brought down from the looms; they were "picked-over" by alert, highly intelligent young women, who removed, or caused to be removed, all blemishes, and then turned the strips over to those whose job it was to assemble, pack and ship them, to warehouse or retailer. The room was quiet and very light, dustless, and I should think much the best room to work in, save for the strong reek of jute and burlap where the packers were. An elderly Scot ran the floor, very ably.

As we drew near to the picking-room, I noticed that my teacher, who was a stalwart man of about thirty, seemed uncomfortable and ill at ease. I could not think what the matter could be; he plainly did not want to enter. Still, the work had to be done; I had to be taught; so he pushed the door and in we went. Instantaneously, the hundred or more young women who were working on the floor looked up to see who was coming in. Instantly, from each throat of all the hundred came a languorous, ironical cry of "Ah . . . there." My poor teacher wilted and blushed; he swore under his breath to keep from weeping, and my own heart went into my boots, for I knew that I could not stand being ragged in that way. In a minute I saw that the mockery was not for me, because some of the bolder sirens swept up and delivered their shot at close range directly to him, with something the effect of firing into an already sinking ship. It was horrible; but I had a gasp of joy that it was not meant for me.

Then a little Englishman who ran that section came up, with the effect of the bull-ring attendants who divert the bull from a wounded man. I never knew

84

why the women were so cruel to my teacher, nor why
he minded their mockery so much. He was not a
shy man; he well held his own with the wits on other
floors. I feel sure that they had some feud with him.
We got away from the floor very soon; my teacher
swore at the women all the way upstairs. A hundred
and more young women at once, against one man; it
is long odds; and my heart sank at the thought that
on the morrow I might have to face those Amazons
alone. A hundred bright young women saying "Ah
. . . there"; it sounds nothing, does it? You try it.

I had to try it next day, alone, as I had feared. My
heart was in my boots as I reached the foot of the stairs;
I need not have bothered; I was only a boy; no pow-
der and shot were wasted on me; just ministering
angels they; only about one said "Ah . . . there"
from force of habit; her cry lacked what Marryat's Mr.
Chucks calls "perpelling power."

Greatly relieved by this, I set about my new task
with energy.

I learned something of the job of mistake-finding in
the first day; it was perplexing to me, for it needed
some knowledge of several processes of which at that
time I knew nothing. I passed my first day of learning, going down to the weaving-floors, looking at carpets on the looms, going to the office for designs, looking at specimen lengths of carpet, comparing these
with the designs, and sometimes bringing occasional
spools to setters, for re-setting. I was puzzled and

anxious at the end of the day. I felt that I had not been a success and that my teacher shared my feeling. I was unhappy about the picking-room and about the many varieties of mistake which I was expected to diagnose. It seemed to me that I was a student sent suddenly to take a general practice in a time of sickness. I felt that half a dozen people would get the wrong mixture and that then I should be sacked.

However, in clearing my mind about this, I took heart. It was a highly responsible job, a real promotion, leading to a good deal more money for books, and certain to make me familiar with every process in use in my end of the mill. It brought me into touch with the weavers at all the different types of loom in use, and with men whose jobs I had not even suspected on the floor above mine. I judged that I could hold the job down, and that I would grind away at chemistry and anatomy in the evenings and save every cent that I could save; then, perhaps, in a while, I could take the plunge and become a medical student.

As I had expected, in a very few hours my teacher was removed from my side; I had to run the job by my own light. This was extraordinarily exhilarating. The work of the day now became a great game of solving puzzle after puzzle, some very easy, some less easy, some most perplexing; and one or two—ah, let us not speak of the one or two; of one at least, by much the worst ever made there. Each puzzle was due of course to the frailty of some worker at some moment, in one or other process. I had to discover, first, what was wrong with the carpet, next, who had done the deed, and then see that it was re-done rightly. It was intricate work, often extraordinarily interesting, as perhaps detective work or research work may be. Sometimes, I would wonder "How on earth has this happened?" Then, patient study would give a clue, and I would see how some weariness, shortness of sight or natural mistake had led from the true path into something very odd.

The work was absorbing; there was a great deal of it; much of it had to be done at speed, however intricate it might prove. Sometimes to-day I glance at carpets on which my feet happen to be resting, and think, as experience will, that carpets are not what they used to be. Often in some modern make of carpet I see this or that which in the mill I should have seen and set right with my own hands. Just beneath me, as I write, there are "a cross" and "a shoved tuft," which ought never to have been allowed to pass.

I will try to describe the work in simple words.

Sometimes, when a new sett was put upon a loom, and the carpet-length began to appear, the weaver would notice something odd, stop the weaving and send for me. These were the glaring cases, the very easy puzzles. Usually, they were due to some reversing of some set of ten spools, or the misplacing of a single spool. These mistakes were very easily put straight, and usually it was not too certain who had done the deed.

In most cases there was nothing which struck the weaver as unusual. He would run off his trial length or "single repeat" of carpet and send it down to the picking-room, where pickers swiftly examined it, marked any doubtful point with a length of scarlet wool drawn through with a packing-needle, and sent the trial piece to me. I then took the carpet design, compared it with the woven piece, and decided which of the doubtful points were mistakes and what had caused them. Most of the mistakes were very small crossings or misplacings of tufts of wool. Usually these were due to the threaders, who passed their days tossing threads of wool over hooks, and were quite certain to cross some of them in the course of the day. I suppose that a good threader handled 25,000 or 30,000 threads of wool in a day, about one a second when a spool was on the tinner. If she were talking to the next girl, or thinking of something else (as I hope she often was), it was easy for her fingers to take the threads in their wrong order. These mistakes were easy to set right. I went at once to the loom, had the chain turned, and re-threaded the misplaced lines myself, or shewed the weaver how to do it.

Sometimes the mistake was more serious, subtler, and more difficult to diagnose. In this case, it was usually due to the setters in the setting-room, who had first translated the lines painted on the design into lines of coloured wool wrapped round spools. It was the custom for setters to work in pairs, one to each half of a spool; sometimes one of them went astray; sometimes they set a line twice, or omitted a line, or set a succession of lines with wrong colours. They set me some perplexing puzzles, first and last; and I hated the moment when the puzzle was made clear, for then there was nothing for it but to stop the weaving, remove the wrongly-set spools, and go up to the poor setters to shew them how they had gone wrong, and leave them to reset what was amiss, which might take them a day or two. I came to know how very difficult some designs were to set, and decided (I think rightly) that these were the bad designs, of intricate pattern and depressing colour. It says a lot for these setters that they never once tried to kill me; and yet, not so; they were devout women, ardent Roman Catholics, who were merry enough on ordinary days, but on all holy days like nuns.

The most difficult mistakes to trace and to correct were those in which wool of a wrong tint had been used in perhaps one of half a dozen strips of a big rug. I discovered at once that over fifteen hundred chief colours were in use, and that to be any good as a mistake-finder I must know them all, with absolute certainty. I know not how many thousands of colours could be had in case of need. Specimens of the chief colours were displayed in a room on the setting-flour, each over its appropriate number. I find it difficult even now to describe the subtle and delicate beauty of some of the colours. I longed to know the miracle by which tints of such poignant perfection could be made in the first instance and then repeated to exactly the same shade. Here were still new, exciting, wonderful processes, which I ought to know, if I were to be of any use. Meanwhile, I had to learn those colours as perfectly as I knew the Rule of the Road at Sea and the Mariner's Compass.

I was a very busy man, when I began this job of mistake-finding; I had much to do and was only fumbling my way into it. During working hours, I had no chance of pausing at the colour-stand to learn a few colours. I had to snatch them colour by colour, and beat each one into my head as the work brought it to my notice. In the lunch time I sometimes learned a few, and at odd times I went over those which I had learned. In time I learned them all. I could look at a line of carpet and name the number of each colour used in it. Possibly for a man this was an average performance; most women would have done it in a week. However, I had not that knowledge at the time, and was not a little pleased at my success. A day or two later, while reading Macaulay I came upon a note describing the workings of his memory. I knew, then, that some men would have looked at those fifteen hundred colours for five minutes, and would have remembered each, by number and by tint, forever.

In a few days I mastered mistake-finding sufficiently to enjoy it very much and do it competently. I was at it all day long, working at speed; well, that was no hardship to me. From childhood, I had been trained to jump to the order; and speed has always seemed to me to be a vital part of efficiency. The continual movement put an end to my day-dreams about the Merchant Service college. I now was moving about all day long, going from floor to floor, stopping a loom, getting another under way, solving some odd error, or causing something to be set right, and having brief words with weavers now and then about the working of their machines. Most of my joy in the work came from its independence. I was the mistake-finder, running the job pretty much as I liked, trusted to do it well, and knowing that I was trusted. The flattery of this was a continual great delight to me; it was my first command, and full of the liveliest interest. No man can be unmoved by the great concerted energy of many men and women. The roaring thundering clang of the energy of the weaving-rooms was a big and exciting thing. Sometimes I felt that it was an enormous dragon and that my mind was going against it with one little purpose, to get at its secret springs and master it. My promotion had not turned my head; it had encouraged me to believe that I could master it. I felt that I had suddenly been lifted to a point from which I could see many of its workings, and begin to understand what lay beyond. What did lie beyond? Where were the brains of this energy? Who was it who knew all the processes which started with blue-flowered flax in the glen and wool on the back of a sheep, and ended up in carpets bought and paid for? I was wondering now at my ignorance of what happened when the carpets left the mill. Somebody somewhere had thought it all out; he had a fleet of lorries, with horses, stables, drivers, grooms. He had warehouses, distributors, travellers. How did you set about selling carpets? How should I set about it? Did you enter a furnishing store with a roll of carpet, unroll it with a flip before some indignant Manager, and at once begin. "Say, this carpet fell plunk from Heaven for you to captivate the prima donna with. Look at the colour-scheme. Tread on it. Give your feet the time of their lives. Roll on it. It's the very bed of love. What? You don't like it? Sir, I never thought to win your discriminating taste at a first effort. Look, therefore, at this second sample . . ."

I knew nothing at all of that side of the business. Somebody, somewhere, was all the time at work on that side of the business, and if he did not do it well, our side of the business might collapse. I was at first daunted by the complexity of the energy needed to make and sell carpets; then the American climate made me feel that there was something grand in mastering that complexity, as well as a kind of fun.

I soon came to know the different types of loom in use. I had often made mats of different kinds of sea. It was very interesting to me to see machinery doing swiftly and certainly what we had done slowly and not very well. Two types of loom interested me profoundly. One was an American type, which wove fabrics so close and good, that they may well be in use to-day. The other was an English type. There were perhaps a dozen looms of this latter type on the lower weaving floor. They wove great, gay, handsome rugs. The mechanism of these English types was unlike anything else. There were things almost like hands in them which caught the great shuttle and hurled it from side to side, as though Djinns were playing catch there. I now judge that the process was wasteful; the thing could have been done more simply; it delighted me at the time. The rugs were superb, only there were never any mistakes in them, to speak of; I seldom had a chance to talk with their weavers. Most of these two types of loom were run by men; the majority of the weavers were women.

I began to feel sure that I could master the mill now that the way was laid open to me. It was a comfort to have confidence; it began to make me feel sure that I could master medicine, too. To be a doctor and to work at yellow fever, that hope shone like a star. I had been brought up in a generation which had suffered much from yellow fever. De Lesseps' Canal scheme had been wrecked by it. Cape Horn was still made necessary by it. I had known many sailors who had seen it at close quarters, and had shuddered at its deadliness and mystery. I had had a friend suddenly killed by it. I longed to work at that enemy, and to help to find "its unseen, small, but million-murdering cause." Very suddenly, I learned that I was not to master the mill, nor to become a scientist; the way of my life was made exceedingly clear to me.

"There was no more to skippen nor to traunce."

On a Friday, the English mail being in, I went, as usual, to the Post Office to ask for letters, and then, also as usual, crossed the road to the bookstore of Mr. William Palmer East, a little further along the avenue. It chanced that he had upon his shelves a row of books of poetry, American and English. In my memory, most of them were the kind of books of poetry which get left upon a bookseller's shelves until someone thinks that one will serve for somebody's birthday. Among them was a Chaucer, price 75 cents, in a dull red binding. I knew nothing of Chaucer, except the old phrases about his being a well of English undefiled and the Father of English Poetry. I bought this book from Mr. East. He said, "Ah, yes, last winter there were lectures on the old poets and Chaucer was asked for. This year it is all the classics, Keats and Shelley."

Those words were very important to me. I had

heard of Keats as a young man in some way associated with Greece (it might be difficult to know less); and though I had heard of Shelley, he was nothing but a name and a quotation. Now these two were named to me as the classics, and I determined to know them. Unfortunately they were not in stock; I ordered both, and hoped to have them in a day or two. I went home with my Chaucer, looked into it, and began to accustom myself to the language. As I had no knowledge of the language I did not sound the final syllables, so that the lines did not scan. However, I saw that he was a lively spirit, providing good entertainment for all hands. I felt that he would be a pleasant companion for the next Sunday afternoon, if I did not walk into the woods.

On that Sunday afternoon, after lunch, I decided not to walk but to read Chaucer. It was a hot, beautiful day; and it seemed a pity to go into the woods while there were still so many mosquitoes. I stretched myself on my bed, and began to read *The Parliament of Fowls;* and with the first lines entered into a world of poetry until then unknown to me.

Many years before, when I was a little child, I had had delight from the early poems of Milton; latterly, I had had delight from *The Piper of Arll.* Now, I tasted something deeper; I was taken into another world, unlike this in its excitement and beauty; it was a new experience.

It seemed to me, that evening, that very likely there

was no limit to the world opened by such poetry; it seemed boundless in liberty, inexhaustible in riches, deathless in beauty, eternal in delight.

The next few days at the mill were unlike others; I had now begun to understand the wealth given to the intellect by thoughtful men. During those days, I came upon the song by Lord Byron, written to Thomas Moore:

> "So, we'll go no more a-roving
>   So late into the night."

I sang it to myself as I went up and down the floors, adding that I was not going to go any more a-roving, save into this new world. . . . Yet I asked myself, "Is it a new world? Possibly it is nothing more than one poem which hit on a sensitive mood. There is but one Chaucer; he may have made only one poem of this sort. I may have to go a-roving pretty far, before I meet with such another."

Within a few days, I came home from Mr. East's store, with two precious volumes bound in dull red, a Keats and a Shelley, both complete American reprints of the Buxton Forman editions, with their notes. I had nothing to do that evening save lie on my bed, under a lamp, and read poetry. I began with the Keats, wondering what a classic would be like, and a little fearful lest it should prove to be in couplets like Pope's Odyssey. I was soon shewn what Keats was like. I read one short poem with amazement,

then a second, which brought me under his spell for
ever, then four lines of a third, and for that night I
could read no more.   I was in a new world where in-
credible beauty was daily bread and breath of life.
Everything that I had read until then seemed like
paving-stones on the path leading to this Paradise;
now I seemed to be in the garden, and the ecstasy was
so great that the joy seemed almost to burn.   I knew,
then, that life is very brief, and that the use of life is
to discover the law of one's being, and to follow that
law, at whatever cost, to the utmost.   I knew then
that Medicine was not the law of my being, but the
shadow of it; and that my law was to follow poetry,
even if I died of it.

Who could mind dying for a thing so fair?

That was the end of my hope of being a doctor; but
by no means the end of my medical studies.   I have
always enjoyed reading medical books and papers, and
talking with doctors.   From time to time, I have
even worked hard at particular branches of medicine;
and have then always regretted not being qualified.
Certain lines of research offer such rewards in benefit
to Man.   There are so many mysteries which need to
be resolved, so many major ailments to be made less
harmful; such weight, mass and mountain of obstinate
stupidity to overcome that even one more willing
helper is worth the having.   Men say that this or that
is the enemy of Life; I say that Death is the enemy;
and he has many friends among men, in all those au-

thorities in whom a debased sense of Life is linked
with temporary power. Their day is like to be long
as I judge; Death does not seem to be threatened yet.

I do not suppose that I slept that night. In the
morning, I opened the volume of Shelley. I had had
one little taste of Shelley in the quotation made by De
Quincey. I turned to the beginning of *The Revolt
of Islam,* from which poem the quotation had been
taken. I only read the first stanza, just to make sure
that this classic were not too like *The Hind and the
Panther,* which someone had told me was a classic. In
De Quincey's quotation the first line of Shelley's Spen-
serian stanza is redundant, and the effect is nothing
out of the way. In the first stanza of the poem, the
second line is redundant, and the effect upon me then
was electric and ecstatic. I told myself that this was
a new kind of verse, such as I had not known existed;
and that such beauty was now going to be with me,
day and night, until I died. What could the trials of
the world matter; the world and its trials seemed illu-
sions, all touched with death; this divine art was Life,
triumphing over death. I went away to the mill, float-
ing as it were on rosy clouds.

The things not touched with joy drop dead out of
memory. That season was a time of radiant joy, for
I went more and more a-roving so late into the night,
into a world of poetry which grew ever greater and
more marvellous as I came to know it more. I knew
nothing of Milton, save those early poems, which had

so charmed my childhood.   I knew nothing of Shakespeare, save two lyrics and part of a short speech.
Once, years before, I had heard a sea captain recite
Marc Antony's oration.   Of course, I had heard and
used many quotations from him, but did not know
that they were his.   I now bought a Shakespeare and
a Milton.   I read the Milton three times through
within the next three months.

All the time, I worked at French poetry, too.   In
studying Villon I came to know D. G. Rossetti, and
thus made my first acquaintance with the Pre-
Raphaelites, who were to be my main delight for years
to come.   William Morris died that autumn.   The
announcement of his death told me of him for the
first time.   I bought his *Volsunga Saga* a day or two
later, and read it with the feeling that it made everything else seem feeble.   Later on, Morris was to sweep
me off my feet with his poetry and prose and to seem
the one sensible man of modern times.

In some way, I had come to know the Essays of William Hazlitt, whose enthusiasm for Burke, Coleridge
and metaphysics, turned me towards metaphysical
reading.   I bought some philosophical books and reviews, and beat my brains upon them, hoping that
they would do my brains good.   Then I started to
read Shelley with the eagerness of youth, and came
upon the Notes to *Queen Mab* and bolted them whole
as revelations of the way of life.

Unfortunately, I read these notes at a time when

their effect could not be countered by criticism. On the very day on which I read them first, I had read in one of my philosophical reviews that none could hope to think good thoughts or do worthy intellectual work without abandoning all food in which life had been. Here were two thinkers, one of them an inspired poet, proclaiming the merits of pure diet, nay, the duty of guarding the temple of the soul from the contamination of the slaughter-house. Feeling that I was filthy with blood and thereby unfit to serve such Queens as the lovely Muses, I decided that I would give up the eating of meat, fish and eggs at once. I debated the point, might milk be drunk? There was a carnal twang about milk; it did not seem quite-quite; yet I decided that I might drink milk, because I loathed it, and that I might certainly drink butter-milk, because that seemed a more loathsome drink, if possible, than the real thing.

The next morning I commenced vegetarian on a very rigid basis. I began to live on bread, oatmeal, vegetables, fruit and milk. I had long since given up the use of tobacco; tea and coffee were now banned; I longed to become a seeing spirit, like Gautama the Enlightened, whose body, though almost transparent, was sufficient shelter and carriage for the soul.

In my enthusiasm for the new life, nothing in the mill could matter to me. I have always delighted in work; I did my day's work well; I was told this when my money was increased, and the praise gave me a great

deal of pleasure; but it was but a part of the ecstasy
in which I was living.   Two quotations were often in
my head.

"Lord of my learning and no land beside" and
"My mind to me a kingdom is."

I had very little learning, few less, but the little
that I had was of an intense joy to me; and to say that
my mind was a kingdom was to understate the case.   I
seemed to possess a limitless universe.

After about a week of vegetarianism, I found that I
had a clearness of mind such as I had never before
known.   It seemed to me, that Shelley had proclaimed
a way of life which might regenerate the world; for
everyone might have the clearness by an act of will;
and in the clearness all things shewed bright or dark,
so that one knew at a glance which were good or evil.
I would sit down in the evenings to write and what I
took to be inspiration descended on me.   To say that
all this was joy is insufficient: it was rapture.

In the height of this mood, at a time which I cannot
now accurately date, a cruel blow fell upon the mill;
we were all suddenly told that the works would close
down for five or six weeks; almost immediately, they
closed.

We did not know the cause of the closing; we
judged, vaguely, that it was due "to the depression,"
whatever that was; the effect upon us all, and upon
the town itself, was black indeed.   If it were true, as

we believed, that between five and six thousand
worked in the mill, then the closing must have stricken
directly at the very lives of twice that number; their
daily bread went at a stroke.   Most of the married
workers could not see beyond the mill; it was their life.
Few of the unmarried men ever saved money.   Few
of either party had expected any horror of the kind;
their ship went from under their feet; and now they
remembered what they had heard of similar cases elsewhere.   In the day or two of panic before the closing,
I heard tales from my fellows of other closings of mills,
elsewhere, not for five or six weeks, but for as many
months, till men were in despair and the pawnshops
refused to take more pledges.

Almost every one of these workers was a willing
active hand, giving faithful return in work for the
good pay given.   It was frightful to me, as it is still,
that any depression or other cause should so threaten
the lives of active willing workers:

"Cannot the mind which made the engine make
    A nobler life than this?"

The blow fell; and I must say, that it taught me how
deep the feeling is of those who have nothing left but
feelings.   Not many people in the world can think, or
want to think, and most of those who do, think
wrongly; but all intense feeling is right.

There we were, caught in a common misery, and

bound to each other by that brotherhood; now brotherhood is one of the greatest of all things.

I have known much most generous kindness from Americans. I shall never forget the universal sympathy in that stricken town; how kind all people were in those days; how gladly they shared what they had, and how tradesmen, the restaurant-keeper, the dairyman, the Chinese laundryman, and two or three more, alike lowered their rates at once, to the cutting-off of all possible profit to themselves, so that their clients should not have too hard a time. I remember some who went to much greater lengths of generosity, by offering to charge nothing for board and lodging: "You can pay me something later, when the mills re-open"; though even this would not have been pressed.

The blow made me take a very careful survey of things. Many of my fellows were afraid that the mill might not open in five or six weeks; I felt sure that it would. I was quite alone in the world there; I had neither commitments nor dependants; I was very well used to hardship of every kind; and had, besides, plenty of money in the bank to tide me over the shoal-water. Still, I felt that it would be wiser to earn than to live upon savings. It occurred to me that I might perhaps be able to ship to the West Indies or Brazil during the time of the closing. I went off at once to the Seamen's Mission in New York, and learned, to my intense delight, that they felt sure that they could ship

me to the West Indies during that week-end, in one
or other of the two ships.

I went to New York for that week-end, with my
gear, and Chaucer and Keats; and there had two
cruel disappointments; "both ships fell down on me."
While in New York on these useless quests, I met a
man engaged in some way in the smuggling of supplies
to the rebels in Cuba. I asked him for a berth. "Son,"
he said, "you're too young for this racket. I want
only family men."

After this, I reflected that I had better stay on at
Yonkers till the mill re-opened; for if I stayed in New
York even a few days more, and then sailed, I might
not be back in time for the re-opening. I therefore
returned, and began upon a month or more of hard
reading and writing, in the first leisure given to me
since I had learned the worth of leisure.

In the house in which I lodged were two men, one
of whom had a complete Dickens and an almost complete Stevenson. All these books were at any service,
and all added much to my delight in those days of
leisure. Soon after the month began, another man
took a room there; he was a fascinating fellow, handsome in a hawklike, Red Indian way, who ran a business of his own, in advertisement of different kinds.
He had been very successful, but his enjoyment was
gambling, and when he first arrived he was silent, and,
as we thought, morose and uncommunicative. Later,
he told us that he had had a run of bad luck at poker,

and that if he had seemed glum it was because he had not eaten for three days together.   Later, we all came to like and admire him.   He was in some ways like the gambler in a Bret Harte story, brave, ready to stake his last cent, generous and square.   He had known a good many cities, and had from time to time written in newspapers.   He had some talent for literary controversy, and had had offers from New York newspapers, which he had rejected, because his instinct was to keep independent in a business entirely his own.   He was exceedingly kind to my beginner's efforts.   He said that he thought that I should certainly be able to make a living by writing "some day," before very long, but that in the meantime I ought to take things more quietly.   He explained that he had lately heard a music-hall actor playing a turn of Edgar Allan Poe raving in a madhouse cell, and that this had struck him as the kind of end a too hard-working poet might expect.

As he was the first man to give me encouragement, I shall ever keep a grateful memory of him.   I suppose he was the typical handsome, generous gambler, whom the world will ever love, who would stake all his having, or his life itself, on the turn of a card or a toss of the dice.   He was not long with us.   He went through the district, for the purpose of his business, and then went on elsewhere.   I heard from him from time to time; and, when letters ceased, I heard of him indirectly, now and then, for many years.

I passed the long leisure, writing and reading. I planned and began a novel, and wrote many poems. One of these poems, through the kindness of a friend in England, was submitted to a real author, whose sole comment was "He writes very young." Well, I was very young. The friend himself gave a more helpful comment: he wrote "Get down from that high horse of yours."

My horse then was the magic horse of brass on which the Tartar king did ride; while he was careering through high Heaven there was no dismounting nor wishing to dismount. I was chasing the comets and finding it fun.

Apart from that riding of the sky, there was little fun in Yonkers at that time for anyone connected with the mill. When the works re-opened at last, the faces shewed too clearly how black a time the closing had been. Even in a land of abundance and prosperity all our thousands had been living on the borders of starvation. What would have happened to us, if the mills had kept closed for a few weeks more? Would it have been reckoned our fault; or "one of the temporary dislocations to which business must ever be subject"; or would someone have wondered, if something were not wrong somewhere with the system? For myself, I knew now what might happen to a mill-worker; I set myself to lay by money against a second shutting-down.

Very soon after the re-opening, a question began

to move the Nation to the very core of its being.

This question was: Will James J. Corbett, the American heavy-weight champion, defeat Robert Fitzsimmons, the English heavy-weight, in their battle on St. Patrick's Day?

As I have briefly told, there had been moments of friction and tension between our two countries in the months before the battle. There was in England at that time an aggressive Imperialism which had left us without many friends among the nations. To many Americans, taught by patriotic school-books, this country seemed the traditional enemy. Generally speaking, Americans were appalled by the manners of our rich and the squalor of our poor. I think that there was a feeling in many minds, that England was "old" and that America was "young" and coming to take her place. This fight was looked upon by many as certain to clinch the matter.

There had been some private bickerings and misunderstandings between the two champions; the Press had seized upon these with much skill; indeed, that able publicist, the American journalist, surpassed himself in the weeks before the battle. I much doubt if anyone in America thought deeply upon any subject except this for weeks together. No modern fight has roused more than a third of such feeling anywhere, even though the rewards of boxers have increased tenfold and cinema and radio have widened the powers of advertisement.

In the mill, national feeling was too pure to admit any doubt of who would win. Even Perce, whose mental life was given to the Ring, and who had ceased to believe in Corbett, would never admit that Fitzsimmons had a chance.

As it happened, I had seen both men in New York. I had seen Corbett on Fifth Avenue acknowledging the cheers of his admirers. He was a beautiful creature, a most lovely splendid man, full of speed and charm and cleverness, with the grace of a panther, and such a look of courage and decision. I had seen him box in one of the little primitive peep-show cinemas, into which you dropped a dime before turning the handle which made the film revolve. I suppose that no more wonderful athlete has ever breathed.

I had seen Fitzsimmons at closer quarters, and had particularly observed him. He was an unusual-looking man, very tall, very big, and ungainly. He had a slouch and a crouch and very long arms. He had a way of moving with a slouch and a crouch which deceived you into thinking of a slow-moving gorilla; then he would straighten up into a very tall straight limber man, with magnificent shoulders, who moved deathly quick. He was pretty bald, he had gingery eyebrows, and a sort of fire in his eye.

Apart from that gleam, the thing which struck me most about his face was the look of collected coolness, which perhaps would not have altered in an earthquake. He looked about as sensitive as a leather bag filled with paving-stones. He was older than Corbett, and was said to be so much slower that Corbett would be in and away before he could move. I had had a good look at him, and felt that he could stand a very great deal of punching, and that his shoulders and long arms gave him a defence not easy to overcome. More than this, he looked dangerous. I felt that in the ring he would become a kind of carroty cobra who would settle the mongoose.

March proceeded towards the 17th with a tension not easy to describe. We talked of nothing else; we read of nothing else. Every man and woman in the mill bought the newspapers that month, and studied the training of the heroes, and prayed that the managers would not let their charges grow stale. The 17th came round at last; we hardly knew how we could get through the day. The result of the fight could not be known till late in the afternoon.

The first reports somehow reached the mill while the battle was in progress; all agreed that Corbett had the advantage and was winning easily. Right at the end of the day the truth was known. It was shouted from the road and repeated up the stairs and along the floors, "Fitz in the fourteenth." One of the boys who swept on my floor burst into tears. He had saved up ten dollars to back Corbett, and now it was gone. I remember one of the elderly women trying to comfort him, with the words "Now ain't that mean"; but there was no comfort for him there.

There have been many championship fights since then, but this one was unusual; even now, after more than forty years, it is sometimes talked of. One man who was there has summed it up to me, "The fight was a corker from start to finish." I still think that Fitzsimmons was lucky to get the decision so early in the fray; I had expected a full twenty-five rounds.

When the mill re-opened after the closing, I used to eat my lunch of bread and fruit with the cutters, propped against a wool-rack. After lunch, I used to read the *New York Sun,* then still under Charles Anderson Dana, to whom I feel my debt to be considerable. In those days he was coming towards the end of his great career. He had received lately that charming and heart-felt tribute from "rare 'Gene Field", who called him "the biggest and the brainiest man" in all New York City. Certainly, the *New York Sun* under his genius had become one of the very best papers in the world. In my memory, I rank it with the *Daily Chronicle,* under Massingham and H. W. Nevinson, and with the *Manchester Guardian* under the late Mr. C. P. Scott.

Charles Dana printed lots of correspondence from people hostile to this country, but he took, as I know now, infinite pains, to shew his readers what was best in English culture and newest in English thought. He was a great lover of poetry; he had gathered to him, on the *Sun,* a number of clever young reviewers who shared his love. Through him, and these bright young men, I came to know all the literary movements of the time, the Regionalist novel-writers, from Thomas Hardy to the Kail-yard School, the Celtic Renascence, as it was called, *The Yellow Book,* the *Savoy,* the Decadents. Now the best of these movements, however much influenced they were by similar stirrings in France or Belgium, were London movements, maintained by writers centred in London. I began to think of London as the centre of the world, where marvellous little companies of comrades met at the restaurants of their sets, to publish little reviews and magazines, which would alter the taste of the time. It was impossible to read those generous, yet discriminating notices in the *Sun* without feeling that London was a nest of singing-birds, a centre of elegance, scholarship, aspiration, joy and glory. All the god-like beings of whom I read, whose exquisite verse was quoted with such tact, were even now living in London; I could see them, perhaps.

I had lately taken to reading Swinburne, who was the first of the moderns, of the men then alive, to come my way. To one who was trying hard to make verses, the revelation of one who could make any kind of verses with this extraordinary skill and delicacy, was overwhelming. I read that this wonderful man, with the green eyes and the shock of red hair, might be seen on any day at Putney, at a house called The Pines, or on a road leading uphill from The Pines towards the Heath.

Then, almost more attractive to the mood of the moment, was the thought of the Celts. I know not quite how the Celts came to hold the position they did. I suppose that some sensitive souls created their image as a counter to the coarse and common images of debased imperialism, then frequent everywhere. At any rate, we began to read, and of course believed, that there were people called Celts, and that there was nothing coarse, common or debased about them, far from it. These Celts lived in Ireland, the west of Scotland and in the islands adjacent, so we were told; and some were still to be found in Wales, though we gathered that Methodism had rather done for them there. Anyhow, wherever they were, they were said to be people of the mists, a doomed race, who went into battle but always fell, who lived (before they went into the battle) in a kind of twilight all their own, in which they communed with spirits. A strange, romantic, visionary lady, named Fiona Macleod, was the writer who best understood these much misunderstood beings, though she, with feminine self-effacement, said that George Meredith was "the Prince of Celts." Well, that was the distinctive work of my decade. I turned to these Celts for fantasy; I had abundance of reality in my daily life. I owe it to the *New York Sun,* that I had the intense joy of Fiona Macleod's romances at the proper time. I began to see, too, that the Celts, and the many young poets, were protesting, by their delicacy and elegance, against the great, sprawling, hideous, filthy apathy of a commercial age.

I used to think, "On Wednesday and Saturday, the . . . and the . . . will sail for Liverpool. If I went in either, I should be in London in ten days' time. I might see the divine brow of Swinburne, wreathed with bay, and the exquisite brow of Fiona, wreathed in mist. What more do I really ask from life?" Presently, when the fair weather began, I took to lunching out of the mill. A walk of a quarter of a mile took me to a little restaurant kept by an old German and his wife, whom I have since nicknamed Mr. and Mrs. Hans Breitmann. Here I used to eat my vegetarian messes of succotash and fruit and drink my milk. I had by this time disciplined myself to such a point that I could drink even a full glass of milk without a shudder. I had come to like butter-milk, and had therefore ceased to drink it; such pampering of the flesh was unworthy of the disciple of Shelley.

The old Germans sometimes told me about Germany. They had left it because they had not liked the change which had come upon the spirit of the people, after their first tastings of profitable bloodshed. Sometimes after lunch, I had time to walk over the little river into sweet wild country not two hundred yards from some of the mill.   Here I could watch the birds, almost all unknown to me, an occasional woodchuck, some wild-flowers and snakes. The river was little more than a brook at most times. Once in that early summer there was a cloud-burst upon the summit of the hill outside the mill's northwestern end.   I was near a window at the time, with one eye on the weather, which has ever deeply interested me.   It seemed to me that the side of the hill was suddenly gouged open, as by a big invisible coulter ten feet broad.   This coulter was the raging rush of water from the cloud-burst; it tore down the hill and across the road, where for some minutes it put the picking-room in danger of being flooded. The flood went on into the river, which became at once a torrent worth the watching.

Afterwards, I went to see the track torn by the water down the hill.   I had not imagined that rain could smite thus.   It had gouged itself a great gutter from the very crest, as though a gigantic waterspout had been played upon it through the nozzle of a hose under a frightful power.

During that early summer, as in the summer before, I used often to walk up the river to Tarrytown and beyond, into wild sweet woodland overlooking the Tappan Zee.   Often, when I saw some yacht or riversteamer going down towards New York I used to think that she was on a road which led without fail to Mersey Bar, where at springs on could count on such and such soundings, see such and such guiding-marks, and come presently into the Sloyne, where friends of mine would be glad to see me. It was hard to watch those ships without wishing that they were bound to the Liverpool River. Often, I thought, "If I knew that such an one were bound for Liverpool, I would swim out to her and beg her to give me a passage." Thinking these thoughts on Sunday made the mill on Monday hard to bear. The truth was, that my months of abstinence had done me great harm. I was beginning to be ill; a day's work fagged me. I did not admit this; but felt, "I am a little out of sorts; it will pass." However, it did not pass, it became worse and though I could do my work and read with rapture afterwards, I was now always wondering whether I could not find work in England a little less hard, say nine hours instead of ten and a quarter, in some city, like London, where the winter would be less harsh, and where there would be museums, art galleries, great lending libraries and reading rooms, and the inspired people of whom my mind was always full. I had come to know that I could not make a life's work there in the mill. I kept telling myself that if I had had more aptitude for it I should have progressed further. I saw little prospect of getting further than I had gone. I was grateful to the mill for having given me a fair chance, and a good measure of trust, with money far beyond my simple needs. But I was sick and homesick, and longed unspeakably for the three or four friends in the Sloyne or homeward bound thither, and for lads of my own age who shared my adoration for Swinburne. If I had had the sense to go to the Restaurant and eat a pound of steak daily for a week my sickness would have vanished, but Shelley was stronger than sense; I wasn't near enough to Death yet, though rapidly hasting to him.

I mention here a thing which seemed very strange to me at the time. One Saturday night in that early Summer, either at the end of May or the beginning of June, I dreamed that I was walking uphill in a deep romantic woodland country quite unknown to me. Presently, in my dream, I found the woodland falling away from the sides of the track, so that there were pastures to my left, and on my right a low hedge of something close, such as lonicera or cotoneaster, shutting in a small, neat, old and very beautiful white frame-house, about which three little girls, in blue dresses, were romping.

It was a very vivid dream; in fact, as a vivid dream will, it seemed much more real than reality.

All that morning, I walked up the Hudson on the East shore road, till I had gone beyond the country known to me. I then turned inland, into an unknown world, and found the land becoming more and more strangely beautiful, until suddenly it became familiar. I said, "This is the country of my dream." I went on, knowing that I had been there, and telling myself what would appear next. The woodland fell away from both sides, shewing the pastures on my left, rather higher than the road, and fenced from it with old palings, just as in the dream. At once, I heard cries of children at play; and there on my right, were three girls in blue frocks playing tag, and the little old frame-house behind its hedge-row.

Not many years ago, on much such a summer day, I tried to find the place. All that countryside has been much changed, from wild, primitive wood and farm, to the outer fringes of a great City. I could find nothing in the least resembling anything in my memory of that strange day's walk.

The splendour of that country in three seasons of the year was something difficult to describe, and always a deep joy to me. I am glad that one of the most beautiful of all its scenes was thus strangely able to impress itself upon me.

My writing, which had been an intense pleasure to me for some months, had now become an anxiety; it was not improving; in some ways, no doubt, it was a good deal worse than it had been. This was partly due to the fact that I was forcing myself to make experiments of one kind or another, usually at the bidding or suggestion of some good writer lately read by me. I had read that one favourite writer

(D. G. Rossetti) read through dictionaries to find what he called "stunning words for poetry"; some of his finds seemed to me so stunning that I was fired to do the like. Another writer advised young people to read dictionaries daily, partly to enlarge and make choice their vocabularies, partly to help them to use the noble words with regard for their precisest meanings. This was sound advice; I recommend it to all young writers. If he had told me to do it wrapped in a wet sheet and standing on my head, I would probably have tried it. I bought a dictionary, and read in it often, sometimes trying to make terser and more telling definitions, sometimes trying to give a more elegant illustration of particular use, and often writing a short passage in which I could display the scalps of the newly captured nouns.

Then I read how Stevenson had played "the sedulous ape" to famous writers; I tried that too, with results so frightful that I will draw a veil.

Then I took to writing imitations, not only of all the forms of verse which delighted me, but of all the forms of verse of which I could find specimens. I tried improvisations. I made verses as I walked or worked. I tried to condense events read in the newspaper into couplets or quatrains which contained the essential facts, and to do this swiftly. I used to marvel and despair at some magical uses of words by great poets. Often, as I walked, I would rack my brain for the words for things seen, the two words which together would make the thing live through time.   I could never find them.

Then I went back to imitating difficult measures, with the melancholy thought that I had nothing of my own to put into the verse-forms when I had learned them.   On Sundays I went steadily on with my novel, and wished that the dull parts might get done, so that I could get my heroine aboard the lugger, whose saucy decks, alas, she never trod.

I remember telling myself: "Even Keats found writing difficult at first; he tried many ways.   No one can put much into early work; he hasn't much to put. Youth is a beastly time to most people, but one grows out of it."

Then I would wonder and wonder what chance I might have in London, of finding something to do connected with books or in a newspaper office.   No chance, I decided; none; yet the thought recurred.

In those days the office of the *New York Herald* was open to the view of all who passed in the street; you could look straight in, and see men whom you supposed to be the godlike editors, sub-editors, leader-writers and reporters, writing their copy as though they would never be old.   To me, it was like looking straight into Paradise.   Always, when I went to New York, I used to see those happy beings, all so much older and cleverer than myself; they looked so happy, they seemed to do it so easily, never blotting a line, and the results next day in the *Herald* completed my despair. It is well possible, that they were not writers, but simply the clerks of the business, keeping the accounts.

When I revisited New York, after many years, I went to see that office, and to look again upon those writers. Alas, that part of New York had been much changed. The office was no longer there.

As the summer began, the thoughts of all Englishmen turned towards London; it was the year of the Diamond Jubilee. All the broad and narrow nationalism in the Empire was deeply stirred at that time; and if the common thing shouted loudest, and was the most heard, the uncommon thing was there, too, in a noble measure.

To myself, in exile, that time was one of poignant feeling. I was English, with no English possession save a few words and a sense of what some had done with them. Night and day, I thought "Over there, at most ten days away, all the English will be holding the greatest festival ever held, to celebrate a time which has left a mark on Time; all the Empire will be there; you ought to go, too." Then prudence with cold sense would say, that possibly a million or two men were thinking those thoughts, that every berth in every ship was filled, and that I should have no chance whatever of working my passage, and an almost certainty of having to pay double for my fare; that I should land in an England completely upset by the rejoicings, business suspended, holidays beginning, and that my lot there might be very difficult.

I kept on with my work at the mill, knowing that cold sense held the cards. Still, hot sense is not so easily laid; my thoughts of England at that time, however incoherent, were passionate enough; they filled my being.

I read the newspaper accounts of all the preparations for the celebration. I worked out the time difference, and kept the hour of the celebration mentally, early one morning. Somebody told me, that day or the next, that the impressive thing in London had been the singing of "God save the Queen" by the crowd, that it had been a noise "greater than any thunder." This thought of a Nation singing stayed with me for many years. No doubt, many of the streets were ahead of or behind others; yet that great irregular sea of sound would come washing up as feeling instead of melody with effects not often known. I have since known them. From that time, I knew that my heart was in England, and that I could not long keep away from her. Even if I were to fail, I should at least fail in England; my life was my own concern and the risks attached to it were for me to take if I thought fit.

I do not know whether that summer were unusually hot. It is always pretty hot in a New York June. In that June there fell some days which affected more of the workers than usual. Often enough on a hot summer day a good many girls and women would faint. If they did not recover, they were sent home in cabs. There came one day of great heat which affected one of the sections of one of the weaving floors very severely. I liked the mill in summer; it was well ventilated and so placed that the blaze of the sun did not fall on the windows. But the sun is the source of energy, and this great burning week filled me with longing to be staking myself upon a die. If I went back to England, I should lose my livelihood, and might well not find another. Against this, I set a proverb, of I know not whom: "There is always life for a live one." If I failed to find anything to do, I should at the least be in England, in my own country, instead of an exile in a foreign land. It seemed most unlikely that I should ever be able to write anything for which anyone would pay me, but then I should at the least be near those friends in the Sloyne; and I felt that even I might conceivably be of use to someone in some way concerned with writing. However, these were flattering thoughts, which I had learned to discourage. Life, as I had found it, was not given to offering what one wanted, but some quite other thing which one was only too glad to snatch. I told myself, that if I went to England I should have a harder time than anything I had yet known. "And yet," I told myself, "even in England boys begin life every day; they find something which they can do. Even in England there must be thousands of things waiting to be done; it ought to be possible to find something." Then I would rebuke myself for looking on the hope instead of on the probability, and yet come back, by day and by night to the hope. Years before, I had read in a Dickens' story the phrase "God's Providence is mine inheritance." I used to think of the Israelites being led out of the land of Egypt. They had a rough passage, and must have regretted Egypt often, but they sought, and at last found. If I did not seek I should never find, but stick on giving my best strength to such work as I was doing and perhaps fall ill and fall out. I was not feeling too well; and I had now a real dread of the New York winter.

Up to a point, I can stand cold pretty well. Unless I am ill, I will write all winter through in a room without a fire. Often, I have sat out of doors writing with the ink freezing on the nib of my pen; this, however, is in England. I did not shrink from the cold in Yonkers; I disliked it, and knew well enough that on certain days in each winter there was death in it. What I did dread and hate in it was the long long shutting down of natural beauty, the death that met the eye, and the grey bones of rocks sticking out of the snow. It is true that the sun shines and puts a magical sparkle everywhere; there was too much snow on the ground and too much ice on the river for too long a time, and my body was giving me a warning that I had worked it and starved it till it was very nearly scrap.

So there I was, longing for England, urged by the blaze of the sun to cast myself on the die and take the chance, feeling that I should not live long if I didn't and might very well die if I did. Cold sense told me all the time, you have a well-paid job here which you do well. It gives you leisure; it gives you books; you can save money on it. Hot sense answered, "the only movement worth anything in Literature now is in London; it would be better to be a proof-reader in a printer's office in that movement than an exile piling up books here until it will be too late."

There was a phrase which I had heard so often from sailors. "Get out of it before the life gets you." Beyond a certain point, no man can escape from a way of life; the life gets him. I meant to get into poetry somehow before the mill got me. Very likely I wasn't good enough for poetry, but the extraordinary beauty of that promised land was enough to call out all my hope and all my courage.

A very slight thing decided me to make the change. I remember well the place and instant of my decision. There was a green swing-door, which shut the picking-room from the staircase. I had passed through this door, and let it swing behind me. I was in the sort of well of the winding staircase, with the stair in front of me and the whitewashed wall on my left.

124

I said to myself, "I must leave this and go back to England."

I went upstairs to the setting-room, where I had a task of some complexity to set right. In that room was a man for whom I had a great admiration; he was one of the best and wisest of all the Americans I have known; and my task had to be set straight by his aid. I said, "I've decided to turn in my job and go back to England."

He said at once, "O, no, John; I wouldn't do that. You've got no job to go to there. You have a good job here. You know, they think a lot of you here. You're on the ladder here. If you stay on, why, you'll very likely have a section before long; and after that, you might even come to have a floor."

I knew that he spoke sense, yet somehow to be writing poetry in a garret seemed a happier fate even than having a floor. I was very fond of this man; he was a splendid fellow; and he had said the words most likely to change my mind. "You know, they think a lot of you here." I had been with them nearly two years and if they thought a lot of me, I thought a lot of them; we had been through the mill together, and they had accepted me. It is not easy to break such ties when the time comes. However, I shook my head, and said, I guessed I would turn it in.

I went down to my section-boss and explained that I was turning-in my job. He said, "Gee, John, I'm sorry." He looked perplexed and perhaps even a little sad. "Well," he went on, "I suppose it's got to be; but I'm sorry; straight, I am. I'd sooner it was anyone, almost, in the section."

A young fellow, who had lately joined the section, heard our conversation; he said to me, "Are you turning-in your job?" I said "Yes." He shook his head and told me the kind of fool I ought to try not to be. "Keep on a job when you got it," he said.

I did not intend to keep on that job; I had finished there. I went up to the office to get what was called "my time," that is, a certificate of the amount of money due to me. I then explained the exact situation of the job I was leaving to my section-boss; the complex mistake had been set straight; the half-dozen other questions from looms were routine. After this, "there was no more to skippen nor to traunce," but to say good-bye to all hands and go. From one of my friends, on my way out, I heard that my floor-boss had said "I shall never have his job so well done again." Sometimes, I think he was right.

I went, first, to the pay-house, to draw my money. It was nearly a mile from the mill proper, I judge. I had never been to that building before, and went to it, now, with some interest, because people had said (I know not with what truth) that somewhere there the designers worked, "with big, expensive kaleidoscopes," to make the designs from which the setters set and the mistake-finders found mistakes. I did not see any designers: I never did; I touched my money and came away.

I went to the Square, to the Bank, and drew out all my savings. I had ample money to pay my passage back to England; but "base is the slave who pays." I meant to work my way, if it could possibly be done. I sent a telegram to the Seamen's Mission, to say that I should be in New York on the morrow, hoping to be shipped. I bought a trunk and some clothes, and went here and there in the town, saying good-bye. Going back to my lodgings, I tore up most of the manuscripts in my possession, many poems and all that had been written of the novel. These, when torn up, filled a large bucket, weighed astonishingly, and burned with a clear flame. I gave away some books, made up a package for the sailors, and sold others for what they would fetch. They fetched a very much larger sum than I had expected. I chose about nine books to take with me; I still have some of them.

All this took some time. It was very hot summer weather, early in July. Early the next morning, I was back in New York, in one of the hottest days I have ever known. In my roving of the world, I have been in very much hotter places than New York. I have been in the Red Sea in September, which was hot enough. I have been in Yuma in July; and it used to be said, that when the toughs died in Yuma they always came back for their blankets. I have been in Death Valley, California, in July, which was the hottest experience I have had. But in almost every summer, New York City will have a day or two I will not say as hot, but as hard to bear, as the world can offer.

That day of my reaching New York was such an one. When I came on to West Street there were several dead dogs and horses lying in the street, all early as it was. I saw two elderly men collapse from the heat as I went to the Mission. In spite of the heat, West Street was full of the bustle and energy of a prosperous thrilling sea-port; the drays and the lorries were plying, with their drivers' cries of Gid Airp; there is nearly always a breeze on West Street, and always flags flying. All the horses were wearing sun-bonnets and ear-flappers. The stevedores, with their bale-hooks, were continually coming across to the Dutchman's, to swallow the biggest schooner on the street, and then return to work. All the ships in that end of West Street seemed to be flying the Blue Peter, which was a glad sight to one eager to be shipped.

In the Mission, they told me to come along, as they felt sure that they could ship me in a cattle-boat just about to sail. There she was, in full view, with Blue Peter flying and a general look of being about to cast off. A stevedore came along, bearing my trunk on his little barrow; he waited on the wharf while we went aboard. She was down to her marks with cattle; she was only waiting for her captain with the clearance papers. We went along an insufferably hot alleyway to the chief officer's cabin. I wondered what it would be like in the cattle decks, where the hundreds of half-mad, terrified cattle, newly beaten aboard, must now be gasping, quaking, and every now and then falling dead.

The chief officer was a most excellent man. He was having a small sarsaparilla with ice in it, under his electric fan. Neither ice nor fan made any difference to the heat. I remember wondering what it would be like in the engine-room. I asked if he could possibly ship me.

He said, "If you'd only come half an hour earlier, I could have given you a pick of three jobs; now, we're full up. But I feel pretty sure you'll have no difficulty further along the street. Try the P—— and the W——." My heart warmed to him, because he seemed eager for me to succeed. He shook my hand and wished me success. I knew that he had to get on deck, to the hundred jobs of a chief about to sail. "Good luck to you," he said.

About a fortnight later, as I was looking at ships in the Queens Dock, before going on board the *Eagle*, I felt my shoulder tapped; there was this excellent man, coming aboard to do his drill. "Aha," he said, "so you beat me here, after all. No; we hadn't a bad time coming over; we lost some beasts from the heat, of course."

When we rejoined the stevedore on the wharf, we debated whether to try the P—— or the W—— next. My companion from the Mission said "We'll get you away today, be sure. You mustn't think of paying your passage until we've tried everything."

The P—— lay nearer to us, but from where we stood I had a view of the W——, a biggish, old-fashioned Liverpool steamer, long familiar to me. I asked, "Who commands the W—— now?"

He said, "Captain T——."

Now Captain T—— was known all over the world to sailors as one of the finest men in the whole Mercantile Marine; my heart leapt, for I knew that he would give me a berth if he had one. "Let us try Captain T——," I said. "All the world knows Captain T——." My companion grinned, for Captain T—— was pretty well known. We moved on through the bustle of the wharves to the foot of the gangway. It was drawing close to sailing time; passengers and their friends were driving up; the stewards were rousing Saratoga trunks on board; the decks were crowded with parties saying farewell; stewards were serving drinks, and journalists were getting copy. We were in some sort of a forward foyer, where people sat fanning themselves or sucking cold drinks. A steward said that Captain T—— was just aft there,

talking to someone. "I'll go and announce you."
As he went, I saw Captain T——, who left his friend
and at once came forward to us.

I said, "Captain T—— I am an old *Conway* and I
want to get back to England. I can pay my passage,
but it would be a great help to me if you could ship
me." "I can ship you," he said, with a grin. "I want
two men, as it happens." He sent a hand below for
one of his crew, who presently appeared and took
me under his wing. I signed on at once; my gear
was handed below; and there I was, shipped. I said
a grateful good-bye to the Mission man, who went
down the side. It was unendurably hot below-decks,
so hot that it seemed impossible that anyone there
could ever be cool again. The ship was crowded,
and all hands were as busy as bees. The time passed
very swiftly. The second needed hand was shipped
before long; he was a young sailor, "going home to
pass." Almost at once, the stewards were going round
shouting "Any more for the shore;" the ship's siren
blew; the gangways were run down into the piers,
and the screws thrashed as the ship sidled away; we
were homeward bound. A few minutes later, I was
at work on deck as we moved down the harbour to
the sea. Though I was busy enough, I looked long
at lower New York, where a few tall buildings (not
what would be called tall today) were among the
wonders of the world of that time. I made some
verses of farewell to them. No man can end a phase

of his life unmoved; I wondered if, and when, and
how, I should see that marvellous town again. However,

> "Men may leve all gamys
> That saylen to St. Jamys."

We were homeward bound and there was much to
be done.

All this happened in another century, in another
world, before the first of the great wars, at a time
when there was some belief in human progress, some
care for the finer kinds of knowledge, and much
apathy and some hostility towards the multitude.

All that way of life is gone, I suppose.

A few winters ago, I revisited the mill. I went up
the stairs so well-known to me, and trod the familiar
floors. The place was then still in use for the making
of carpets, but the system had changed beyond all
belief. I dare say that process after process had been
made more simple or avoided by one clever device after another. The mill which had roared and
clanged with a deafening din was now so quiet that
one could talk in the weaving-rooms. The hundreds
of workers were no longer there, and yet the place
was busy, even very busy. The looms had changed.
I did not recognize any part of the machinery in use.
I went to a big strange machine which was making
carpet. It was in the section where I had often talked
to a weaver called Dunk. The weaver told me that

this was the kind of loom they used now. It was probably a much better machine than any I had seen or helped to work; it did not make a noise. I wished that I could stay there to get the hang of it, but I was now only a visitor. It occurred to me, that I was the only visitor I had ever seen there.

The great building seemed empty of inhabitants. This seemed wrong. The cheerful crowd had been exhilarating; except on the holy days the floors had been merry with laughter, chaff and chatter; and perhaps everybody had felt the excitement of being there for a common purpose, of thinking that each was contributing something to a thing which did not yet exist, but would become a carpet through the united effort. I have felt this excitement from time to time in newspaper offices, where all met nightly to produce something which could only exist through what we did.

Well, the factory system as I saw it is dead apparently, except in my memory. It is of little use to say what seemed amiss long ago; but one who has been through the mill may be able to say what would have been good long ago. When the present war is at an end, a good deal, that ought to have been made good long ago, may tempt some impatient souls to violence. I repeat, that I have nothing but gratitude towards the mill; it gave me a square deal, with ample pay for a good day's work, and the leisure for which I had longed for years; it gave me a chance to study.

In the twenty-two months of my time there, I heard no complaint and no growl from any day-worker. Some of the piece-workers said, though not angrily, that if they made too much money their rates were reduced, so that it never paid them to work too hard. For the day-workers, the discipline of the mill was up to sea standards, men had to work or go; well, no one objects to that; the slacker and the knave are better out of a mill than in it; we gave a square deal in return for one.

When the mill closed down, after it re-opened, and only at those times, I heard voiced the feeling that something was wrong. Nobody knew what was wrong; nobody allotted blame to anyone; but all felt, that something blindly and greatly wrong had come down upon their helpless poverty, and that such wrongs should not be. They did not know how to prevent the wrongs; they were incoherent, thoughtless, unpractical; but they were sufferers, have no doubt of that, and in their dumb way cried for justice.

Of course, the main political effort of the last forty years has been to stop that kind of wrong and to render justice to such criers.

I was very lucky, in seeing the factory system in a land which held very strongly the concepts of equality and of dignity; there was a very strong feeling in America, that no life should fall beneath a certain standard.

In lands without that feeling the factory system

began without forethought and proceeded without mercy, producing violence, ruin and a waste of strength not easy to be reckoned. In those lands, it was proclaimed that the business man, the hard-headed practical business man, was the one to do a piece of work. But those who saw him at his work were forced to wonder if such an one had any practical sense whatever. He had the faculty, it is true, of getting a crowd of unfortunates to work for him on the lowest possible terms, and produced by their means a number of ill-made, ill-designed, cheap things and a smaller number of much better-made, but much worse-designed, expensive things; he allowed his workers to live in what dens they could, he sacked them when he wished; he made no provision for their age, and paid them so meanly that they could make none for themselves. When he thought fit, he sold or closed his business, and retired with a clear conscience.

That type of man has probably ceased everywhere; the bitterness the type roused has poisoned the worker's mind for a hundred years. That type of man is the real cause of poverty, which does not come from below but from above, from somebody in authority with a debased view of life. He is always the source of the poison, which runs swiftly down, stunting and blasting with stupidity, more stupidity and complete stupidity, instead of health, wit, joy and rapture.

If you had compared the United States of forty-five

years ago with any other country in the world, you would have said that they had no poverty. There was no degradation of life there; there were no "Poor," the starved, stunted, ill-clad, untaught off-spring of untaught, ill-clad, stunted, starved parents.

There was, however, plenty of uncertainty in the life of even the American worker, prosperous as he was compared with his European brother. This uncertainty was felt by all the married hands, who often talked with me of the things which would have cheered their lot.

Well, what would have seemed good in the mill, all those years ago? First and foremost, some arrangement or provision against unavoidable sickness or accident; some defence against any closing of the business, through depression or bankruptcy; every worker felt exposed to these horrors and helpless when they came.

There may have been Friendly Societies and similar palliatives at work in those days; men wanted something backed by the State, they knew not well what, except that they felt a life of honest work to be good service to the State, deserving such recognition, as help in sickness, disaster, and old age.

Some of them were uneasy, lest their jobs should be lost by some invention or simplicity of process which would make them unnecessary. Among inventive people with much mechanical talent, this happens frequently; a new machine may cut out the

work of ten men; what is to become of those ten?
Find new jobs? They may have spent twenty years
doing the jobs now ended; they may be less quick to
learn; and less attractive to the foremen in need of
hands.

One or two men, interested in labour problems,
have asked me: Did the hands feel bitterly, at passing their days in making or helping to make, carpets
much too expensive for themselves to afford?

I say: No, not in any way. They were Americans,
certain of two things, first that they were in every
way as good as those who could afford them; and,
next, that if they hustled and made good, they themselves would be able to afford them. They were de-
fended, first, by dignity, then, by hope; and these
two comforts, long denied to many European workers
are by no means small.

If people will consider them carefully, they will see
that they are fundamental in any state and society;
they are the foundations on which to build.

I am sure that many young men in the mill, who
wished to learn the processes and be of use to the
craft, would have welcomed, and used in their spare
time or in the lunch-interval, some museum or show-
room making plain the making of carpets, shewing
the methods in use, from the earliest times until the
present, and encouraging study, comment and criticism. If we had had series of ten-minute lectures,
from designers, dyers, weavers, setters, sellers, buy-

ers, etc., they would have been eagerly attended; we would have paid to hear them; and beyond doubt would have done better work, through taking more interest in what we did.   I, who was a reader, should have been glad of a technical lending library attached to the mill, though this would have had much less general success than a set of museum models and a series of talks.

Looking back upon the time, I feel that much might have been done to make the work more exciting, interesting and delightful.   Honest work is a delight in itself; but delight in the work can be added to honesty.   Our work was honest; the workers' honour was as marked as among sailors, who often, in those days, would not so much as sharpen their knives during a watch on deck, from the feeling that that would take them from the work they had pledged themselves to do.

Honesty must be the foundation of all work; but no work can be counted really good till it uses the lively and lovely qualities in the worker.   Those qualities were not used in us.   Our work was a wrestler whom each of us tackled every day and put down upon the mat before the whistle blew.   It was an opponent whom we beat by strength; not a personal friend to take pride in.

At sea, men could always take pride in their craft. I do not mean the ship, for no man can fail to love a ship and give her service almost as to a living thing;

I mean the details of that service which depend on personal skill. What sailor has not loved getting a beautiful skin and bunt on to a furl; or having all yards square by the lifts and braces; or having his brass like gold, new points on his ropes-ends, Turk's heads on his staunchions, and mattings on his hatchway rails? Every boy in a ship has some opportunity for craft of these kinds, or for petty command of some sort, such as responsibility for a duty, a part of the ship, a place or boat or piece of rigging, each bringing a pride and a chance to give of the very best within one. These things were not in the mill; and the life was the poorer for their lack.

I have read of carpet-makers, in distant lands, whose carpets were designed and made by entire families, who worked on each one for years together and put into the work all that they had of wisdom, knowledge and delight. I have looked at such carpets in museums, sometimes for an hour together, without coming to the end of my wonder at the depth of feeling in the work. My fellows and I helped to make many miles of carpet, possibly some hundreds of miles during the time that I was there. In how many of the designs of those carpets did we take any interest whatever? We were engaged for all our working day on carpets; how many of their thousands of festoons and zigzags stirred a depth of feeling in us?

I, personally, never saw, and never wished to see, more than half a dozen of the completed works. One very complex and costly piece gave me a great deal of careful work; and I was glad to see its component strips safely off the looms and assembled. I had to watch it in all its stages, and it was interesting to me; the chance, that I was the mistake-finder, made this possible for me. Dozens of strips of design passed through my section daily, in their spool-stages. How many of them did my fellows go to see upon the looms? or try to see when completed?

I think that I am right in saying that they went to see one, and one only. I was told that the carpet-designers of the nineties used "big, expensive kaleidoscopes" to obtain suggestions of pattern and colour. I never met any carpet-designers, nor saw them at work; I cannot tell if they used kaleidoscopes or not. From my memory of the designs, I should say that in the past, say, in the eighteen-seventies, most carpet-designers used kaleidoscopes a good deal. Towards 1885 or so, the teachings of Ruskin, "that the artist should observe Nature and study natural form," began to influence designers everywhere. From my memory of the designs, I should say that the kaleidoscope became thenceforward a less trusted friend; it was not thrown aside, but its odd, angular, unmistakable pattern was now often graced with some pale blue roses or a spray of violet ivy speckled with yellow. Sometimes the roses were red or yellow, or black or brown; often they were tied with ribbons which trailed all over the carpet; and often the ivy was scar-

let or some other colour. I do not know that Ruskin
would have admitted that the results were due to his
teachings, but I believe that they were.

When I was in the mill, that kind of carpet was
frequent all over the world; you might say, that most
of the carpets woven bore designs of the sort. Sometimes, the colours were agreeable, but in nearly every
case the designs were uninteresting to the eye and
mind. Remember, that the carpets were designed
to lie upon floors, to be trodden under foot, and perhaps not much noticed.

Now whatever perverted fun the designers may
have had with them I believe that no setter on earth
could take pleasure in setting such designs, no worker
would want to see the results appearing on the loom,
no weaver could be glad to have helped to make them
carpet, and no picker would remember the results
beyond to-morrow. In short, there was something in
the designs, such as deadness of invention, or something wanting in them, of living delight, which made
all those who worked to make them carpet, apathetic
if not hostile.

It is said that cooks do not greatly care for food,
that jam-makers never touch jam, and that the seaman's dream is ever of a farm. But artists and craftsmen love the things of their work above all things,
with passion and care. We in the mill, were all
craftsmen and potential artists, the separation of hand
from soul, which went on daily, by this parting of the

designer from the weaver, was in every way deplorable. So far as we knew, no designer ever saw his work upon a loom or went to see it finished in the picking-room; he never talked with a setter nor with a weaver. He cared, seemingly, as little for our work as we for his.

If we had been in touch with each other, we could have told him that his sense of colour was this or that, his twirligig-border absurd, and his main design a dreariness to the minds which had to dwell upon it. If we had little sense of design, we had, at least, vitality, which was what he mostly lacked.

Of course, the best work of any time is very good. All through the nineties the looms of civilisation turned out some works of great splendour, rather more work of great gaiety, and some of delicate beauty, including varieties of plain-cloth, of enchanting colour. We, in the mill, turned out some work which we all knew to be superb in its strength and finish. I know that men went from my section to particular looms just to see and to touch that noble web, and to taste the delight of knowing that no weaving anywhere could be better done. They relished the honest, solid work; they saw themselves in that.

Now there was one design in use in the Yonkers mill which roused the keenest possible interest on four of the floors. It is not easy to rouse the keenest possible interest in four or five hundred young men and women; but I write this with sober thought, stating the fact, which seems to me to be of great importance. The design was for a small rug, of the hearth-rug size. It spiritedly represented a Fox running away with a fowl. Like most designs, it was probably set in different tones, but when I saw it the lively act was done in gay colours. It was said to be an old design; it might, even, have been very old, fifty years or so. Its effect upon the workers of four floors was profound. Unfortunately, I do not know if it affected the pickers as deeply as the rest. I first heard of this design soon after I entered the mill. One of the cutters said, "Ah, they ought to be setting the Fox again; that's some carpet, The Fox." Other men spoke upon hearing of the loved design. When the Fox had last been done, they had had delight in their work, they had pulled their weight in the making of a work of art; the memory of that joy had endured. When I saw the design, after hearing so much about it, I did not like it. I am afraid that I then preferred the kaleidoscope's octagons, linked with festoons of blue roses in yellow baskets.

When the word went forth that The Fox was being set, a thrill ran through all the sections. The women who set it loved every line of it; they delighted in their work. The threaders perhaps were less excited, but the cutters cheered when the setts came up to their knives. When they were put on the looms everybody in my section found some excuse to slip down to the weaving-room to see the vivid scene hanging like a picture before them. "Gee, boys, that is some carpet; the good old Fox again."

From the first, I had felt that the place of carpets was on the wall, as tapestry and story telling. There is no need whatever for the putting of elaborate design beneath people's feet, plain-cloth suffices, or would in every way be better. I have often thought of that design of the fox, and have repented my old scorn of it. The instinct of my fellow-workers was a lot sounder than mine, they demanded action in a work of art, and by their instinct saw that nine tenths or more of the designs they helped to spread were without interest.

If the mill had been making woven pictures for wall-decorations, as well as plain-cloth for floors, the work would have been of an absorbing interest to all in my building. The setters of plain-cloth would have done their work without any anxiety or nervous strain; they could have taken a week at plain-cloth, perhaps, after three weeks of picture-setting; they would have found the simple task a rest. The setters of the pictures, after seeing the design in its entirety and understanding the fable, would all have gone about their task with an eagerness which they could never feel for the coloured twirligigs that were their usual portion. To myself, who care for stories, work in the making of these histories would have been a continual delight.

Only fifty years before, the wall-paper makers of the United States had been making landscape and sea-scape wall-papers of extraordinary beauty and interest. In their way, for small rooms, these are perfect for walls. For large rooms, I still maintain that a woven picture, which has not to be glazed, is the next best decoration to a fresco. If we had been weaving scenes from American History instead of meaningless twists of impossible vegetation (if it were vegetation) all hands would have been happy all day long. The completion of one length of one sett would have been an event in the mill; the watching of it through the loom an excitement of a new kind, and the putting together of the lengths into the completed fable a thrilling joy to perhaps fifty workers and a deep interest to hundreds more. It would have brought a keenness into the mill which might have embarrassed the management.

Of course, some critics have replied, "There was no demand for that kind of thing": "The public didn't want that kind of thing": "Any work of that sort would just have been left on the dealer's hands, and the mills would have closed down."

How is a "demand" for a kind of carpet made known? How does the public show that it "wants" a kind of carpet? How many wealthy people, potential patrons of art, "want" any particular kind of carpet and insist on having it designed and woven, to their wishes? How many intelligent people, the natural critics of design, refuse the wares offered? Is it not the case, that there is no "demand," no public want, whatever, but certain shrewd and plausible sellers, who will blarney the somewhat flustered and foolish buyer into taking anything they want to sell?

Of course, it often happens that even the most persuasive seller cannot sell certain carpets; they are left to be sold at one of the Annual Sales, under the legends "Great Reduction," "Sacrifice Price," "Must be sold to clear," etc. The seller must not keep his stock too long, for the ways of life of the idle are subject to a tyrant called fashion, which may for all that I know, be but another word for a plausible seller persuading foolish, flustered buyers into taking what he has to sell.

Having looked through thousands of old designs, I judge that the fashion in carpets changes fairly quickly. In the nineties, the fashion was changing for the better. Ruskin and William Morris had bettered all the arts of design throughout the world, and the wave of improvement was still in flood. Yet in most mills throughout the world carpet-designers were designing carpets without reference to the workers or the buyers; carpet-buyers were taking carpets at the bidding of sellers who knew neither the designers nor the workers; and carpet-workers, completely indifferent to designers, buyers and sellers, and never coming into touch with any of them, spent their days in mechanical tasks with all the energy and beauty of their fantasy neglected, unused and sometimes mocked and outraged. This state of things was due to "the hard-headed, practical business man"; and a melancholy mess it was.

I know that some maintain that no art of any kind can come from the working man. That is nonsense. Art is nothing but delightful work; what else is it? Art is the work of healthy men with lively delight in what they do. In the general mess due to years of war, the arts of design seem to be worsening. It may be that the few remaining rich people have ceased to buy modern carpets. I think that they more frequently pay dealers to buy them ancient Turkish or Persian rugs, which will be liker what their rivals have and more certain to fetch money if things become worse. More people buy plain-cloth than formerly; and some kinds of floor-cover have been invented which serve rather well, with a mat or two, instead of carpet. In shop windows I sometimes see kaleidoscope-patterns mixed with yellower, greener and bluer apple-blossom than ever soothed the feet of the Victorian. I saw an appalling one today: its effect was very chaste, if by chastity you mean the complete annulment of design.

Carpets are an improvement upon the litter of bones, shells and bits of meat of the cave-dweller, the bare earth of Odysseus' palace, or the rushes and filth of the mediæval hall; they are not likely to cease among us. I feel sure that Nature shews us the ideal carpet in the grass, in the sea-sand, or the sand of the desert, all, mainly, plain-cloth of agreeable colour. Carpet-makers have many exquisite colours; they had 1500 chief colours forty-five years ago, they must have many thousands more now. You may have too much of some good things, but never of good colour. Even if nearly all carpets were plain-cloth, two thousand different colours would offer a marvellous variety.

Everybody in a northern climate, such as ours, needs a carpet or a rug upon the floor for more than half of each year. There are enough wools, yarns, looms and hands in the Empire to provide everyone with a sufficiency of carpet; can it be said that there is not the will, too? If everybody were to have a carpet, the weavers might feel assured that their mills would not close down. Let it not be thought that I would limit any craft to one type of work, or check the divine art of designing. Carpets can be superb works of art. I have seen some amazing modern works on the floors of some of the greater Mahometan Mosques. I would love to see works of similar quality on the floors of great halls and foyers here. There is endless room for the play of fantasy and delight in the planning of mats and hearth-rugs. I still maintain that there is a great field for the big woven wall-decoration. I would love to see this take the place of the coloured glass window in our churches; the temptation to smash would be so greatly lessened.

Might it not also hide the baldness of the average wall in the average municipal building?

Handicraft teachers have assured me that a good many people come forward each year "interested in textiles." Why should not these join a textile service in youth, and be carefully trained for it? It is true that textile-making is work, not sport; but why should not textile-making be more delightful than sport? I maintain that it is infinitely more delightful than any form of sport, involves and exercises greater qualities of mind, and produces something of benefit to everybody. All sports involve training of some sort; why should so many works remain haphazard? Whose are the haphazard minds in high places, the minds without enlightenment, without keen sympathy, the muddled and muddling minds who keep us in our muddles?

If carpets are worth doing at all, they are worth doing well. Good work in any art or craft is due to special aptitude or genius linked to a skill which can only be acquired by toil. It is very important that those in any art or craft should meet each other frequently in youth, for discussion and for the kindling of mind with mind. Probably our school-teachers would have little difficulty in choosing from the scholars leaving school in each year the few hundreds of recruits eager to enter the textile service. These should not be caught by the industry at haphazard, as in the present time, but recommended, after their own inclinations have been seen, and then trained at various processes of the craft, firstly to test the inclination, and then to discover the special aptitude. In the training, which should be very thorough, every means should be taken to make the candidate a better specimen, bodily and mentally. In the training, those with no skill or interest could be weeded out into other work, in which they might show one or other.

William Morris turned many minds towards handicraft, and said his vigorous say about his commercial age. I have met a good many of his disciples, some of whom were amateur weavers, who made their own designs, did competent work, and had a lot of pleasure in it. At sea, I made a good deal of primitive sword-matting, and know, from that, what fun they had and have. I have sometimes heard amateur weavers speak as though their work were more honest and better than the work of the power-loom. This seems to me to be bunkum. A good power-loom will make easily and swiftly a web which will last a century; it will weave yards while the hand-loom potters at an inch. The power-loom is a superb and splendid servant. Of course man, latterly, has used all his machines to destroy some element of his humanity.

William Morris was right in insisting that Art grows out of work. It is surely best when it grows out of the strength and interest of many happy men

in the comradeship of creation. In the carpet-mills
of the future I hope to see the setters, cutters and
weavers competing eagerly or collaborating joyously
in the making of exquisite gay designs which will
give them all delight and make their work-day a
joy-day. Very soon, these will ask the great designer
to make for their joint work some superb design
which men will come to see for centuries.

I cannot be sufficiently thankful that in my childhood I met some of the last of the choicest craftsmen
of the sea, and learned from them what joy a day's
work can be when it is lifted into art. They knew,
that it takes time and a lot of trouble to point a rope,
yet they pointed all their running rigging, as a matter of course. They knew, that it would take time
and trouble to make the broad bunt-gaskets for
courses and topsails, yet they made them, and then
found that they would not look well, unless the bunt
were triced-up by a specially roven jigger, and perhaps dropped a dozen times at each furl; yet, what
matter, the result was beauty, and to themselves deep
joy.

I suppose that the worst thing about the last century's factory system was its haphazardry. The people entered it as they could, without training and
without aptitude; "they found a job," as they said;
they asked nothing more from life, which was then
exceedingly unpleasant if they failed. They generally found the job early in their teens, when they

were much too young to be looking ahead, or to have thought out a way for themselves. It is best to have a way for yourself, to have your own canoe and to paddle it your own way; then, if you go over Niagara, you go down in command, with an unobstructed view of the Fall. Consider the waste, the indifference to personal genius, the neglect of any attempt to discover what each citizen may become good at, in a haphazardry of the sort. A licence so to exploit the young was given to every hard-headed practical business man throughout civilisation; the stunting of mind was done wholesale; the blunting and narrowing of talent was practised on nations at a time.

This haphazardry beset the average worker throughout life. When it had brought him into industry it often flung him out, through no fault of his own, in what was called "the returning cycle of economic depression." He then entered what was called "the pool of labour." Sometimes one saw the members of the pool singing in the streets, or walking dejectedly to some distant town where, as they had heard, some work might be had.

These were honest good men, sober, skilled, hard-working; a thing called a depression, a stupidity made by stupidity, caused such men not to be wanted by their community. I ask again, with the great poet:

"Cannot the mind that made the engine make
A nobler life than this?"

If I refer frequently to the sea, it is because so much of sea-life shews possible solutions of labour problems. One of the great charms of the life at sea is its variety. Surely, one of the drawbacks of factory life is its frequent monotony.

Thinking over the days in the mill, I feel sure that the older men would have benefited by a change of work. Most of the processes were easily learned, and most of the men would have welcomed a change, as very refreshing. In a perfectly ordered industry, a tired pattern-weaver would change to plain-cloth, a setter with fantasy would try a month of designing, and be all the better for it. The Americans have made much of the institution of the Sabbatical Year, in which the Seventh Year is given to students for travel and study. This institution would be of supreme benefit to industry. The business man asks: Where is the money to come from? It comes from the profits earned by the business so improved. Besides, the "business" of the future need not be concerned with money but with getting the world's work done with pleasure to the worker and profit to the community. The wealth of a land is not money, but healthy, wise delightful citizens, fond of books, arts and games, and having high standards of behaviour. These things can be had by good will, by the will to have them, not by money.

Sometimes, a writer or a politician will use the phrase "the Ship of State," as though a country and her people were like a ship and her company. They are not. A country and her people are always infinitely worse off than a ship and crew. A ship is built and equipped to a plan clearly thought out. A State is a haphazard nondescript always being patched up somehow for present use. A ship has a purpose for which she has been designed, her crew is properly subdivided, after examination, some to direct, some to do, some to supply the others. A State has usually no purpose whatever; when she has, it is usually something baser than would be permitted to any individual citizen; such as the murder of some neighbour. Whatever subdivisions may be made in her people may be unmade overnight. A ship, if she puts to sea, does so after examination of her fitness, after the filling up of stores, completion of crew, loading of cargo and ballast. She goes with intent "towards" a known destination. The State does not even know for more than a week together if she be a monarchy, a dictatorship, a democracy or some modern mixture of the three; still less can she know if she be a trader, a man of war, a store-ship or a sheer-hulk like old Tom Bowling.

To one who has known the order of a ship, it must seem desirable that a State should be liker a ship, with a trained, properly subdivided crew, a port of destination, a course set towards that port, and care taken against possible dangers. A State is like a ship, in that she may meet with enemies, and ought to be always armed, with the best modern skill (not the best skill of twenty years before), in self-protection. As the wise American said, "You may not ever need a gun; in a decent world, you ought never to need a gun; but, if you DO need a gun, you'll need it so badly, you'll be glad to have it." A State is like a ship in that she has a population which needs food; she ought always to have within herself an abundance and certainty of home-raised food; her duty towards her population is, that each of the citizens shall be fed.

To this extent, certainly, a State ought to resemble a ship; a ship, that is, fit for heroes, such as Odysseus' ship or the Pelican.

Might it not also be a good thing to settle a course, to decide what the State is for, what it is to try to do, what its aim is to be?

While I was working at the mill, at least two English factory-owners were trying to make model villages or settlements about their factories. They did well what all should have tried to do.

No such attempt was then being made in America; there was no need, because the conditions were so much better and the standards so much higher. The cheap immigrant was on the spot, of course, with his much lower standard; the American knew that within a very few years, the cheap immigrant would either raise his standard to the native level or return to Europe. There was an immigrants' quarter at Yonkers;

it looked pretty tough. Apart from this, the surroundings were seemly, and within a few minutes' walk of sublime natural beauty. There was no need for any "model village": we had one. If our Directors had built us a model village, most of the hands would have been puzzled and perhaps just a little indignant. Still, I am all for order, plan and beauty. The factory-owner in many lands has been free to use and misuse men without any such things, and his misuse of the land has poisoned and made hideous many thousands of fair acres. There is really no reason why a factory and its workers' homes should not be as fair to the eye as a College, or Mediæval Abbey. Men will give reverent service to beautiful places; they enjoy working for Colleges, Abbeys, ships. In my wanderings, I have lived near very hideous places, where the work done was not enjoyed and the service was not so much given as forced. Where there is squalor, slavery is not far off.

Unfortunately, the efforts of the two English pioneers have not established a new order. In spite of the success and grace of what they did, every country in the world has defiled its beauty with factories and factory towns as ugly as hells upon earth. What we see, when we look at them, is not mean, dirty, squalid building, but the image of a mind which we have put into authority.

In trying to set down the story of my time in the mill, I have found that for most of the time there was no story; all my life was lived outside the mill or deep within myself. The time ended nearly forty-four years ago, and much of it has dropped from memory. I was very young then, and youth is a time of unhappiness. I was very unhappy, from youth, exile, home-sickness, the worry over a friend, and despair of being able to master the fates which offered and attracted. I was also unspeakably, radiantly and burningly happy. I had found my road. It was a deep time, such as one would not be without.

If one were to ask, "Would I have that time again?" I should answer, that one time of youth is sufficient for one life. If, as some think, it be our lot to undergo other youth, let us hope that wisdom learned in this life may save us then from our mistakes and those of others.

Often, I hated the mill; sometimes in dream, I have thought that I had to be there again, or was there again, unable to leave, and have wakened glad to find it not so. When I revisited it a few winters ago, my heart sank at the sight of it, and I knew again my old winter horror.

As I went in, that fell from me wholly. I hoped to see some of my old companions and to hear about the rest. Surely, some of the twenty, whose talk and lunches I had shared for nearly two years, would be there still. In this I was disappointed; they were gone; and I felt chilly and grown old.

Whatever the time was or was not, those men were

my friends and companions. They made allowances
for me, they taught me my jobs; we saved each other
from trouble many and many a time. More than
this, we did many a rousing good day's work together,
and the bond between us was still strong.

Even if they be all dead, as I fear, I dedicate this
book to them. I remember one of them saying,
"John is English, but we take him in as one of the
people." I hope that I shewed my gratitude to them
then; I declare it now.

JOHN MASEFIELD

Oxford, 1941.